Shameless Persistence

Lessons from a Modern Miracle

SANDRA BRETTING

To Shadina,
I hope the Lord
speaks to you
through this!
~ Sandra

Higher Ground Books & Media
Springfield, Ohio.
http://www.highergroundbooksandmedia.com

Printed in the United States of America 2019

Shameless Persistence

Lessons from a Modern Miracle

SANDRA BRETTING

"…if you keep knocking long enough, he will get up and give you whatever you need because of your shameless persistence."

Luke 11:8, New Living Translation (NLT)

Table of Contents

Introduction

How many times have you been asked to pray for someone and thought, “Here I go again?”

Maybe it’s for someone’s physical healing. Or his financial situation. Perhaps someone’s made a bad life choice and now she’s suffering the consequences. (The infamous “unspoken prayer request.”)

Whatever it is, sometimes prayer fatigue sets in. *What’s the point? What difference does it make? I probably won’t even find out what happens to him or her.*

And sometimes that’s exactly what happens. We pray for days, for weeks, for months, even, but we never see an answer to our prayers. We wonder whether God still hears us, or whether he even cares.

Then, he startles us awake. He performs a miracle right before our eyes, at a pace that takes our breath away.

Do you need a shot of adrenaline today to bring your prayer life back into focus? A reason to believe you’re not wasting your time? Some real-life examples to bolster your faith in prayer?

I hope you find it here, and more. Because my story shows how God works through the prayers of his people. How he heard their cries over one icy weekend in Houston, when more than a thousand Christians came together to rattle the gates of heaven on my behalf.

Sometimes, the people who prayed over me didn’t even know my name.

Chapter 1: AND SO IT BEGINS

I never set out to be a medical miracle. I never *wanted* to be a medical miracle. But sometimes, what we want and what God wants are two very different things.

Like many people mentioned in the Bible, God chose someone perfectly ordinary that day when he reached down from heaven in January 2018. Just another fifty-five-year-old suburban wife and mother who lived on the outskirts of Houston, Texas, with her family.

My posse included a husband of almost thirty years (Roger), two daughters (Brooke and Dana), and a slaphappy rescue dog with more brawn than brains (Chance).

Brooke had recently married her college sweetheart and moved to Dallas to pursue a career. Meanwhile, Dana lived at home while she wrapped up her senior year of high school and applied to colleges both near and far.

Life was pretty good, to be honest. Ever since I graduated from The University of Missouri School of Journalism in 1985, I'd wanted to be a writer. I'd freelanced for newspapers like the *Los Angeles Times*, when I still lived in California, and then for the *Houston Chronicle,* when our family moved to Texas for Roger's career.

Deep down, though, I wanted to write mysteries; my favorite kind of books. After taking a zillion creative writing classes and reading even more rejection letters, God finally granted me a publishing contract in 2012. I wrote one hardcover mystery, and then another. By 2015, I had a six-book contract with a New York publisher to write something called "cozy mysteries," which are soft-boiled stories that dial down the sex and violence. I was right in the middle of writing my fifth book in the series when Baby New Year arrived in 2018.

In other words, I had a loving husband (check), a job I'd always wanted (check) and two amazing daughters. (Check, check.) Life wasn't perfect, but it was close enough.

Does that sound familiar? The Bible is full of people like

me…ordinary people with everyday lives, who chug blissfully along until God upends everything in one fell stroke.

Consider the prophet Jonah. He lived in a mountaintop village about eight-hundred years before Christ was born. Jonah had everything going for him: a close community of family and friends; access to both the Sea of Galilee and the Mediterranean Sea; and a respectable career as an oracle for God.

What he didn't have was a desire to preach to the Israelites' sworn enemy, the Assyrians. So, when God called him to do that very thing in a city called Nineveh, he balked. Several calamitous detours later, including one inside the smelly stomach of a fish, he finally got with God's program and got his life back on track.

While nothing quite so dramatic happened to me, I felt very much like Jonah pre-Assyrians: blissfully unaware things could ever change.

Until the morning of January 17, 2018, when I woke up feeling "not quite right." I'd been suffering from lower back pain for a few days, but I passed it off to a wonky spinal cord that acted up every now and again.

Like most days, I rose at six o'clock and waited for the sun to appear, so I could walk our rescue dog around the neighborhood. Roger sometimes joined us on these treks, but he was doing business in California that week, so Chance and I were on our own.

Now, my dog lives for his morning walks. He usually sits by the kitchen table until sunlight cracks the night sky, and then he throws me dirty looks while I finish my coffee. It's as if he's got a cartoon bubble over his head: "Is it time? Is it time NOW? C'mon. It's gotta be time now."

Only, Chance didn't do that on January 17. He stayed in his bed and quietly watched me from the corner of his eye. People who believe dogs have a special sense about sickness are no doubt right. It was as if Chance knew I was sick, and he knew he had to be on his best doggie behavior that day.

By the time pink sun glinted off the ground, the ache in my back had become the least of my worries. I threw up once, and then again. My cheeks burned. Although I didn't use a thermometer, I suspected a fever.

Luckily, Dana slept upstairs while I debated my options, since the Katy Independent School District had cancelled classes for the day. A freak ice storm the night before had caked the roads with sleet and left them nearly impassable.

Two hours later that day, though, I started to shiver, and I felt like I was walking through fire, then ice, and then fire again. *This isn't good.* Maybe I'd wake up Dana after all, so she could drive me to an urgent care center for a rapid flu test or a scan of my lower back.

While she got dressed, I "googled" the nearest urgent care center, which happened to open at nine o'clock. Then I grabbed a trashcan from my bathroom and headed for the garage. Even with a raging fever, I didn't want to bother the center's staff by throwing up in the middle of their clean waiting room.

A few minutes later, Dana and I hit the road in her Kia. Sure enough, icy patches covered the streets, particularly the midsection, where tires wouldn't reach. An eerie quiet surrounded us, as if the entire city had evacuated the night before, but no one bothered to tell us about it.

We arrived at the urgent care center a little before nine o'clock. For some reason, ours was the only car in the parking lot. I hugged the trashcan to my chest and thanked God for our good fortune, since I wanted to be first in line when the center opened.

My euphoria lasted only a few seconds, until a four-door sedan pulled up next to us. Now we had a competitor for the number-one spot, so I urged Dana to try the clinic's front door, just in case. *No dice.* She hurried back to the Kia, and I silently prayed the next car over would be polite and let us go first when someone finally unlocked the door.

Once the dashboard clock crept past nine-fifteen, Dana checked the center's website on her phone and discovered the storm had shuttered the clinic until noon. *What now?*

Little did we know God already had performed a small miracle. He knew I needed more than an urgent care center could offer, and he knew I would've wasted precious minutes—if not more—had it been open. What seemed to me a nuisance at the time was actually a blessing in disguise.

Our only other option was an emergency room, although I

hated to spend that kind of money for five days' worth of Tamiflu or a simple CT scan. Like most mothers, I cringed whenever someone else fussed over me, since I'm usually the caregiver.

The ache in my back silenced my protests, though, and I mumbled some vague directions about driving down the road to the nearest emergency room, not even sure of the hospital's name. Several well-known medical centers operate satellite hospitals in Katy, and I figured Dana would pick the closest one.

Which brought us to miracle number two. Being seventeen, Dana had no idea which hospital to choose. She'd suffered bumps and scrapes over the years, but nothing serious. She pulled out of the parking lot anyway and gamely headed down the feeder road, the black Kia rolling over the ice like a hockey puck sliding toward a distant goal.

She ignored me when I suggested a certain hospital and drove the Kia into the parking lot of Houston Methodist West Hospital. Although Dana didn't know it at the time, God had guided her to one of the best hospitals in our city…a place where every nurse wanted to work; where every therapist scrambled to get placed; and where all the top doctors practiced. The hospital's staff didn't just follow the latest medical protocols; they wrote them. I crumbled out of the car the moment we arrived and stumbled into the ER's waiting room.

Uh- oh. Unlike the urgent care center, three other families waited ahead of us, their sick or injured tightly wrapped in fleece blankets. No one would look at each other, because we all knew we were competing for the next available spot. I settled into an industrial plastic chair near the reception desk, and, every so often, I'd feel someone's gaze flit my way, as another patient silently weighed her odds against mine.

My heart leapt when a nurse called me first. *I won!* My joy lasted a split second, though, until I realized being called first in an emergency room was *not* a good thing, no matter how good it felt at the time.

Dana helped me shuffle to the registration desk, where I settled into yet another industrial plastic chair and a nurse slid a fancy thermometer across my forehead.

For some reason, she frowned when the reading appeared. She tried again, only this time she ran the thermometer across the other side of my forehead. Now a confused squint appeared. She gamely tried a third time, before she gave up and lowered the device.

104 degrees, she whispered. She sounded both awed and horrified at the same time.

A wheelchair magically appeared at my side, and an attendant helped me move into it. Beige walls slid past as we all maneuvered down the hall, the sharp smell of antiseptic trailing after us.

The attendant steered the wheelchair into a draped cubicle, where a nurse helped me change and moved me onto a paper-covered gurney. People came and went—a rainbow of different-colored scrubs depending on their jobs—as they checked vital signs, listened to my account of the morning's events, and corroborated my story with Dana, who sat across from me. By this point, Dana had contacted her dad, and he scrambled halfway across the country to get an earlier flight home.

The minutes crawled by. Time has no meaning when there isn't a clock nearby. Sounds reached through the curtains, though: the squeak of tennis shoes on rubbery linoleum. Whispers—sometimes urgent, sometimes not—as disembodied voices discussed a patient in the next cubicle over. The soft beep of a machine above me that squawked whenever one of my levels fell too low.

By three-fifteen, doctors had a name for my problem. Based on things like my temperature and low heart rate, they suspected sepsis. The word meant nothing to me, until a physician explained how serious it can be.

Sepsis is an extreme reaction to infection. To fight the intruder, our bodies sometimes release chemicals into the bloodstream, but those chemicals inflame the organs and interrupt the flow of blood, which causes the organs to fail.

About two-hundred and fifty-thousand people die from sepsis in America every year, according to the Centers for

Disease Control. [1] The worst form is abdominal sepsis—which I had—where more than seventy-two percent of patients don't make it.

Fortunately, the doctor left out that last tidbit, so I wasn't too concerned with the diagnosis. I still thought maybe I had a kidney stone or something equally benign. Especially when the doctor ordered a CT scan around dinnertime and a kidney stone the size of a black-eyed pea appeared near my upper left kidney. The image was cloudy, though, and ghostly swirls of white painted the areas meant to be black.

Later, when I read my medical chart, which ultimately ballooned to one-hundred and twenty-three pages, I found a note posted by the attending physician: "Anticipated length of stay is one to two days."

Everyone believed him, of course. But only because no one realized how deadly those feathery swirls of white would be.

---

[1] The Mayo Clinic Patient Care & Health Information, updated Nov. 18, 2017

Chapter 2: BAD GOES TO WORSE

I spent the night in the medical-surgical unit strapped to bags of IV antibiotics, lactic acid and other indistinguishable fluids. Meanwhile, Roger tried to rest on a stiff pull-out couch next to the bed, his dress shirt crinkling like rice paper as the night wore on.

A nurse checked my blood oxygenation level every few hours, which hovered at ninety-seven percent. It wasn't a great score, but she'd seen worse.

Roger gamely greeted me the next morning, his eyes bruised from the lack of sleep. Today was the day I'd have the kidney stone removed. Since the hospital normally discharged patients by four o'clock in the afternoon, I'd be home in plenty of time for dinner, right?

But the surgery didn't go as planned. With so much infection, the urologist had no choice but to drain my kidney and bladder, rather than worry about the four-millimeter stone lodged nearby.

I don't like to discuss things like scabs, mucous or blood, but the urologist—a gentle giant with a wry smile—didn't mince words when he spoke to my husband after the surgery. He said so much pus filled my abdomen, he could barely insert a stent there to drain it all away.

By noon on Thursday, I groggily awoke in the OR recovery room with a brand-new Double J stent lodged between my bladder and kidney. I fidgeted uncomfortably as the anesthesia wore off. Unlike the emergency room yesterday, the air in this recovery room seemed thinner; weightless. I couldn't inhale enough of it to satisfy my lungs.

My breathing grew more labored. By now, my blood oxygenation level had fallen to eighty-five percent. A nurse replaced the cannula, which was a thin tube that leaked air from an oxygen cannister to my nose, with a thick plastic mask that covered half my face. Even with the change, I still couldn't breathe.

Losing your breath is a strange thing. It focuses your thoughts on something that should be automatic. Imagine suddenly realizing you couldn't blink your eyes or wiggle your toes. All you want to do after that is close your eyelids or move your big toe back and forth.

Someone should really check on the air in here, I remembered thinking as I sucked in the manufactured air. *Maybe there's a hiccup with the oxygen machine.* Otherwise, my lungs would contract and expand like gangbusters, given the amount of air being forced into them.

**Take a moment to inhale deeply. Once…twice…three times. Feels good, doesn't it? I'll never take the ability to breathe for granted again. Too many people rely on machines to breathe for them, and they'd trade anything in the world for one clean gulp of air.*

The hours dragged on, and still I couldn't breathe. An ER nurse finally asked for permission to wheel me to the intensive care unit on the second floor and I meekly agreed, knowing deep down things were spiraling out of control.

By this time, Roger had called my two sisters to let them know what'd happened. My older sister, Elizabeth, worked as a special-events planner with Focus On The Family in Colorado Springs, and Roger caught her right in the middle of hosting a program for donors in Washington, D.C. She immediately passed the event over to someone else, and then she booked the next available flight to Houston.

The journey was a bit quicker for my younger sister, Cori. She managed her husband's dental practice in a town near Austin, about three hours away. Cori arrived in Houston later that afternoon and stood by Roger in the ICU as my vital signs weakened.

Now, my blood oxygenation level dipped to seventy-eight percent. Then seventy-five. Seventy-one percent. By seven o'clock that night, doctors had a name for my newest problem: I'd developed acute respiratory distress syndrome (ARDS).

The odds of my survival plummeted. To confirm the diagnosis, an X-ray tech performed an emergency scan in the wee hours of Friday morning. Most people's lungs are bone dry when they're scanned. But sepsis, along with the fluids used to cure it, had infiltrated my body and muscled out the oxygen. Without air, my organs couldn't survive.

The news devastated Roger. One of his best friends from college had died because of ARDS while still in his twenties. Greg never regained consciousness after doctors put him into a medically induced coma to save his lungs.

Back when Roger's friend was alive, in the late nineteen-eighties, the survival rate for ARDS patients was only eight percent. Today, that number is closer to fifty percent. While still not great, it's a sevenfold increase, thanks to more research, better technology and improved medical protocols.

But ARDS wasn't my only enemy, and when combined with sepsis, it delivered a one-two punch to my lungs. At four-forty that morning, while the rest of the world slept outside my hospital window, the staff put me on life support. Once again, my odds fell when fluid spurted everywhere as the physician did his best to thread a tube down my trachea.

The doctors were running out of options. Here they'd placed me on one-hundred percent oxygen, and still it wasn't enough. Too much fluid had washed through my lungs, and a scan taken an hour-and-a-half later showed even more clouds in my chest than ever before.

The double whammy of sepsis and ARDS had thrown my body into a freefall…and even the best hospital and physicians couldn't stop it.

Chapter 3: A DEATH SENTENCE

Few people driving along Interstate 10 that morning probably noticed a light that glowed in a hospital window above them. If they happened to catch the soft orb as they whizzed past, they might've thought a new mother was up with her infant. Or, maybe a grandfather couldn't sleep, so he worked a crossword puzzle while he waited for his breakfast tray to arrive. Maybe someone who worked nights forgot to extinguish a desk lamp before she finished her shift.

The commuter couldn't possibly know who really stood in the half-light of room Twenty-Fourteen: two men dressed in scrubs, one on either side of a hospital gurney, with a gut-wrenching message to deliver.

It's time to call the rest of your family and let them say goodbye.

The words tumbled through the air, end over end, horribly solid and wholly irretrievable. Just one simple sentence. Spoken in a whisper to my husband and sister.

As if the moment wasn't surreal enough, one of the men turned sideways, so my family wouldn't see him cry. He wept with his head ducked because he didn't want to upset them even more.

The unthinkable had happened. What began with vague, flu-like symptoms had escalated over just two days into a fight that couldn't be won. First came a kidney infection, which turned to sepsis, which triggered ARDS. It was a chain reaction that no amount of manmade oxygen or Lasix (the trade name for a medicine that pulls fluid from the body) or any other human intervention could stop.

Imagine a house of cards, perfectly still on a coffee table, until someone touches the first card. Slowly, the house begins to wobble. As soon as the card leans against its neighbor, the weight of them both takes down a third. And so on, and so on, until the only thing left is a pile of rubble.

Roger called our daughters first. He woke Brooke up as

she lay sleeping in Dallas, his words split by sobs. She threw on some clothes, kissed her new husband goodbye and pointed her car south for the four-hour drive to Houston.

Dana hadn't slept much to begin with. Ever since she brought me to the emergency room on Wednesday, one day had blurred into the next as she traveled back and forth between the hospital and our home. She, too, quickly dressed and headed for the ICU.

But in that moment, when Roger couldn't speak, when he could barely catch his breath, he used his cell phone one more time. He typed out a short message, which he texted to a friend. He didn't agonize over the words, or how to phrase them. He just sent a few simple sentences that ended up changing everything: *Please pray for Sandy. It doesn't look good.*

When someone delivers news like that, we say it "spreads like wildfire." As if our words could ignite a match that smolders to a flame. To me, that text was more like the *crack* of a billiard ball that hit a triangle of stripes and solids and sent them careening in every direction.

Because that's exactly what happened. While my medical team frantically infused me with even more medicine, Roger's news *cracked* over the wires and onto the screen of his best-friend's phone.

He numbly pocketed the cell afterward. He didn't provide any details, and he didn't explain why. He didn't even mention a look that passed between the doctor and a nurse only a moment before; a look he wasn't supposed to see. The physician had ordered even more Lasix, which I wasn't due to have for another three hours, and then he slowly arched an eyebrow as if to say, "What difference does it make? We're losing her anyway."

Meanwhile, a few miles away, Roger's friend read the text and prayed. He didn't struggle with the words, either. As soon as he said amen, he texted another buddy with the same prayer request. *Crack.* And then a few more. *Crack, crack.* The balls began to roll in every direction as news spread among our friends and family.

Dana arrived at the hospital first, followed by Brooke. Although I don't remember it now, people tell me I cried when I saw my girls, because I knew exactly why they were there.

More texts and prayers followed. Dana contacted the prayer team at Kingsland Baptist Church, our home church at the time, along with Hope City, a brand-new church that met in local high schools. Someone else contacted Second Baptist Church, which is one of the largest churches in Houston, with more than sixty-thousand members and six far-flung campuses.

The news continued to *crack.* Once they prayed, several friends hopped in their cars and traveled down ice-slickened roads to reach the hospital. Just a few people at first, drawn by the need to see and touch and comfort my family. Then a few more. Brooke's former college roommates from Baylor University drove in from Waco…Austin…Dallas. Dana's buddies bolted through the doors of Taylor High School the minute the last bell rang and headed for the hospital.

I can only imagine what ICU staffers thought as Friday waned and people began to fill the waiting room. Even Elizabeth made it there by nightfall, the conference in Washington, D.C., a distant memory by now.

Every time the elevator doors whooshed open on the hospital's second floor, another friend or neighbor or Bible study leader stepped out of it. *Crack.*

People formed a tight circle with their chairs, and when they ran out of those, they sprawled across the industrial carpet and shared cups of Starbucks coffee. The sound of people praying, chatting, of crying, even, filled the room. Some people arrived at the hospital within a few minutes, while others traveled hours to get there.

One friend was right in the middle of dinner with her family at B.J.'s Restaurant in Clear Lake when she heard the news. The server had just deposited a pizookie, which is a cookie-cake the size of a small pizza, on their table. My friend let her family enjoy one brief bite, and then she told them the news: they needed to drive to Katy, more than an hour away. Everyone thought she was joking—who leaves behind a perfectly good pizookie?—until she convinced them otherwise.

I can only imagine what the scene looked like in the ICU waiting room that night. People holding hands…praying…hugging my family when words failed them. I like to think that Satan's demons, if any clung to the rafters that night, quickly fled when the room began to fill with so many Christians. How could they compete with that?

As Friday night morphed into Saturday morning, people slowly dispersed. Some returned to my house to sleep. Others, like my sisters, took turns sleeping on the paper-thin carpet in the waiting room, or in a plastic chair by my bed. My daughters did the same, grabbing whatever rest they could between the *beep*s and *buzz*es and *shriek*s of monitors all around them.

Roger spent the night staring at the bedside monitor as my vital signs ping-ponged all over the place. My heart rate zoomed dangerously high, and then bottomed out again. My blood pressure continued to fall. And, every time the night staff thought my oxygen intake couldn't get any worse, it did.

My urologist—the one who had such a hard time scrubbing the infection from my kidneys—stopped by my room several times that night.

"I've been doing this for fifteen years," he later said. "I know what happens when people have your kind of readings. They don't survive it. There's no way they can."

Meanwhile, news continued to spread in our community, and elsewhere, as Saturday morning dawned. A church in Kennett, Missouri, asked its members to pray for someone more than six-hundred miles away, thanks to a phone call from a friend who had relatives in the area. Details were vague: a mother in east Texas was on life support and wasn't expected to last the weekend. The same thing happened with churches in Louisiana. Mississippi. California.

All in all, more than a thousand Christians prayed over me that weekend. Their individual prayers rose over the spires of local churches, seeped from the east-facing windows of nearby synagogues, and then drifted up from the shingled roofs of family homes miles and miles away.

One of my favorite stories involved St. Basil the Great Greek Orthodox Church, here in Houston. Another friend asked its members to pray for me, which they did…in Greek. Now, I don't speak Greek, and I can barely understand it when it's spoken to me. But I imagine even the angels stopped to listen that day when those Texas Christians beseeched God in their native tongue.

And while God's people rattled the gates of heaven on my behalf, an X-ray tech once more wheeled a portable scanner into room Twenty-Fourteen. This time, the image showed a paper-thin sliver of empty space in my left lung. It was the first good news since my family was told it was time to say goodbye.

The hours passed as my body rallied. By Sunday morning, the fluorescent peaks and valleys on the bedside monitor flattened, until the lines looked less like mountaintops and more like rounded hills. More time elapsed between alarms. Doctors and nurses began to back away from my bedside, no longer worried they'd lose me at any moment.

Meanwhile, people came and went in the ICU waiting room. Every one of them remained focused on a single mission: to pray me back to life.

Throughout Sunday, my vital signs grew stronger. My blood pressure rose little by little…first to seventy systolic, then eighty. Another chest X-ray on Sunday night showed the fluid had cleared from two-thirds of my lungs.

All this time, an oxygen tube still snaked down my throat and cuffs shackled my wrists to the bedrails. By Monday morning, I'd apparently had enough of *that*, so I pretended to sleep, and then I waited for everyone to tiptoe from the room. I inched my face as close as possible to my right hand, and then I whipped out the tube in a single, fluid motion.

Apparently, I'm not the first person to take out her own tube in an ICU, and I surely won't be the last. Respiratory therapists even have a name for it: ICU delirium. Some studies show up to fourteen percent of all ICU patients on ventilators take out their own tubes. At least I have *that* in my corner whenever a doctor reads my chart and gives me a funny look afterward.

With the tube out of my trachea, the respiratory staff now reconsidered my need for it. Back went an oxygen mask over my face. More good news: my lungs were clear, so I could once more return to the medical-surgical unit on the fifth floor.

It felt so good to put the ICU behind me as I traveled three floors higher. In my new home-away-from-home, code blues rarely broke the quiet, teams of people didn't routinely rush down the hall, and no one spoke in hushed whispers whenever they passed a patient's room.

As a matter of fact, I got to know the staff on the fifth floor pretty well over the next few days. There was Otillia, a sweet nurse who called me "baby" and gave the world's best sponge baths. Another nurse named Rain, who decorated the white board on the wall with fanciful storm clouds and whimsical splashes. My doctors, of course. Brilliant men and women. One of my favorites was an internist—a man of science with thirty years' experience—who confessed that prayer often made the difference between his patients who survived ARDS and those who didn't.

"I do my best, and then I leave the rest to God," he said, with a shrug.

After ten days in the hospital, at least eight bedside chest X-rays, and a whole pharmacy's worth of medicine, it was finally time to go home. Nurses, therapists and doctors filed by my room at the end of the week to say good-bye. Most thought I wouldn't make it. They were the ones who cried happy tears when I rose from the bed; who shook their heads when I shuffled down the hall; who beamed from ear to ear as the elevator door *whooshed* closed behind me for a final time.

At the beginning of our journey, Roger had whispered something to me: he wanted us to walk out of the hospital together, hand in hand. He didn't know how, and he didn't know when, but he was going to take my palm in his and together we'd step into the sunshine.

Sure enough, at four o'clock on Friday, January 26, my husband and I held hands as we moved from the lobby of the hospital to the parking lot. It was a cloudy, gray day, but neither of us cared.

And once the machines fell silent, once an IV bag no longer pumped medicine into my veins, once another patient with a different diagnosis moved into room Twenty-Fourteen in the ICU, it was time to acknowledge the truth: God had orchestrated my recovery; something no doctor, medicine or machine could do. He'd heard the prayers of his people, and he worked a miracle few people expected to see.

The ordeal has since changed me in a number of ways. For one thing, I learned more about prayer than I ever knew before. It's one of the greatest gifts God has given us, but it's something we don't always understand. Or, we grow weary of doing it, and we end up mouthing words we don't necessarily believe.

I'll never forget a friend who approached me about a month after I was discharged from the hospital. With tears in her eyes, she asked me to forgive her. She wanted to do so much for me, she explained, but all she could do was pray. As if that wasn't enough. As if she should've visited my hospital room, or brought me some flowers, or cooked a hot meal for my family, for heaven's sake.

In truth, what she did was *more* important. She gave me the greatest gift of all: she spoke to God on my behalf when I couldn't say a word.

What could be better about my prayer life today?

____
____
____
____
____
____

What are three things I could be praying for but aren't?

1. ____
   ____
   ____
2. ____
   ____
   ____
3. ____
   ____
   ____

How could my prayers impact a friend/neighbor/family member/coworker?

____
____
____
____

Chapter 4: WHO, ME?

It's so easy for our prayer life to fall into a rut. After a while, it becomes routine, like feeding the family dog or brushing our teeth. Morning after morning, night after night, day after day. Brush, rinse, spit. Repeat.

When we say our prayers, they usually spool out in the same way. We might thank God for the day we've had, or the day ahead of us, and then we ask him to "bless" our family and friends. (Whatever that means.) We'll add a few sentences about a sick neighbor or a fellow churchgoer, picking and choosing among the people we know. (And usually, the people we like.) Then, we either hop out of bed to grab a cup of coffee, or we yawn "amen" and nod off for the night.

At least, that's how I used to pray before I became sick. I never really thought my prayers would change much of anything, so I approached them as a chore, not a privilege. After all, my friends and family know lots of people, and I wouldn't be the only one praying for them, so what difference did it make? Other people would pick up the slack, and quite frankly, they might do a better job of it than me.

Only that's not what the Bible says about praying for others.

In James 5:16, the author explicitly tells Christians to lift each other up with prayer, and why. He doesn't qualify his words with "sometimes," or "convenient," or "occasionally."

Confess your sins to each other and pray for each other so that you may be healed. The earnest prayer of a righteous person has great power and produces wonderful results.[2]

Although scholars don't know for sure which James wrote

[2] James 5:16, New Living Translation (NLT)

the book (there are two possibilities), many people attribute it to James, the half-brother of Jesus. If so, this was a man who didn't even believe Jesus was the son of God until he saw him resurrected.

As the disciple John noted when he detailed the many miracles Jesus performed:

For even his brothers didn't believe in him.[3]

That is, until Jesus walked out of the tomb after three days. At which point James became an ardent believer and began to exhort Christians to cover each other with prayer.

The Bible is full of stories about people who prayed for a friend or loved one and saw wonderful things happen because of it.

In Acts 12, an entire church gathered to pray for the disciple Peter. He'd already been imprisoned by the Sanhedrin once and escaped with the help of an angel, but then King Herod Agrippa had him arrested again and bound in chains. (Herod couldn't risk another embarrassing prison break, so he made sure Peter had twice the chains and sixteen prison guards this time.)

So Peter was kept in prison, but the church was earnestly praying to God for him.[4]

Imagine the surprise of the people who gathered at Mary's house to pray when Peter showed up on the doorstep that night, again having been led out of prison by an angel. The poor servant girl who answered the door was so excited, she forgot to let Peter in!

When she recognized Peter's voice, she was so overjoyed she ran back without opening it and exclaimed, "Peter is at the

---

[3] John 7:5, NLT

[4] Acts 12:5, New International Version (NIV)

door!" [5]

Fast-forward fourteen-hundred years, to the cobblestone alleys of Medieval Europe instead of the dusty streets of Jerusalem. There, men and women were allowed to purchase a little something called "indulgences" from the Roman Catholic Church. The indulgence was supposed to shorten the time they (or a loved one) spent in purgatory, and Pope Leo X had just tossed out a new batch of them to pay for a fancy basilica.

It was a win-win for everyone: parishioners who participated bought a clean conscience, the Pope got a surefire source for new revenue, and the church got its cathedral.

Only…a certain teacher and theologian by the name of Martin Luther didn't see it that way. He not only called it unbiblical, but he thought the practice weakened peoples' faith. He wrote up his objections in the *95 Theses,* which he nailed to the door of Wittenberg Chapel. It was the first cannon-shot in a war between the church and the German theologian, which ultimately led to the Protestant Reformation.

Quite an accomplishment for someone who didn't have access to Instagram or Facebook, who couldn't advertise on TV or radio, and who'd never heard of a P.R. plan.

Whenever people talk about Martin Luther today, they no doubt picture a towering, forceful personality. The truth was much different. Martin Luther was a sickly man who suffered from a host of physical ailments during his life, including depression, and it only got worse as he aged.

He often wrote to his best friend, another theologian by the name of Philip Melanchthon, about his poor health. After a particularly bad spell, he wrote: "I spent more than a week in death and hell. My entire body was in pain, and I still tremble. Completely abandoned by Christ, I labored under the vacillations and storms of desperation and blasphemy against God. But through the prayers of the saints [his friends], God began to have mercy on me and pulled my soul from the inferno below."

---

[5] Acts 12:14, NIV

This was a man who changed the course of religious history; who flew in the face of the Roman Catholic Church; who dared challenge the Pope himself. But some mornings, Martin Luther couldn't even get out of bed.

What if his friends had decided they didn't need to pray for him? After all, he complained to them all the time, and they probably got tired of hearing about it. They might've rolled their eyes when a new letter arrived, because they knew it'd be chockfull of complaints about dizzy spells, poor eyesight, and ringing in the ears.

Maybe they wished he'd just snap out of it. Pull himself up by his bootstraps and go back to teaching at the University of Wittenberg, where he belonged. Stop clogging their mailboxes with the latest litany of his health problems.

Not only that, but this hypochondriac was a celebrity. First in Germany, and then the rest of Europe. News of the teacher who was brave enough—or foolish enough, depending on one's opinion—to challenge the church rippled over the continent. His ideas no doubt touched off a million dinner-table discussions about what it meant to be saved by grace.

His notoriety meant hordes of people probably prayed for him. Why wouldn't they? He was revered as a saint in some quarters, and his fans no doubt continually asked God to protect him from the naysayers.

So, his friends easily could've begged off the "chore." They could've reasoned their time was better spent studying the Bible or formulating their own ideas about faith and the afterlife.

But they didn't do that. Martin's friends prayed for him anyway, which gave him the strength to continue teaching and writing. In fact, he wrote one of his most famous hymns, "A Mighty Fortress is Our God," during that time:

A mighty fortress is our God, A bulwark never failing;
Our shelter He, amid the flood Of mortal ills prevailing.
For still our ancient foe Doth seek to work us woe;
His craft and pow'r are great, And, armed with cruel hate,
On earth is not his equal.

Without the prayers of his friends, there's no telling

whether Martin Luther would've been able to pen those words. He didn't think so, and he knew his circumstances better than anyone.

The famous thinker behind the Protestant Reformation was just one example of a man who relied on the prayers of his friends to get him through dark times. Friends who didn't flinch when he requested their prayers; who didn't justify their refusal by citing the hordes of people who already were praying for him; and who didn't put their own needs above his.

Which brings us to another point. Have you ever been asked to pray for someone, only it's someone with whom you're not on the best of terms? Maybe you've had a disagreement with him, and there's still a bad taste in your mouth from your last conversation. Or, you think she's made some poor life choices, and you're not surprised when she runs into trouble. What if it's someone who's said hurtful things *to* you, or *about* you? Whatever the circumstances, you feel less than chartable when it comes to praying for that person.

Don't worry, you're not alone. Before my hospitalization, I had a run-in someone who purposefully omitted me from a very important event. It was painful to be excluded, and I harbored a grudge against this woman for several months. To be honest, praying for her didn't even enter my mind. But then something interesting happened. After my physicians moved me out of the ICU and into a room on the general-surgical wing, I thought about our spat, and how silly it all seemed. The argument was so petty and such a waste of time, given what had happened, I vowed to let it go and pray for her instead.

Maybe you've got a bigger reason to begrudge someone your prayers. Maybe the person in your life has hurt you in a more profound way. But that still doesn't mean it's okay to exclude them from your prayers. In fact, they might need your prayers more than ever.

A perfect example comes from a terrible shooting that happened in Alexandria, Virginia, in 2017. Each year, members of Congress play a softball game called the Congressional Baseball Game for Charity. One team consists of Republican congressmen and senators, while the other includes only Democrats.

On June 14, 2017, at the last practice of the season, the

Republican team met at Eugene Simpson Stadium Park, which is about five miles away from the Capitol. U.S. Representative Steve Scalise, a Republican from Louisiana, manned second base while his teammates warmed up in the field.

Suddenly, shots rang out and Scalise dropped to the ground in agony. Someone had fired a shotgun at the players, which shattered Scalise's pelvis and femur, and caused massive internal injuries. The congressman pulled himself to the dugout with bullets whizzing overhead, where his teammates yanked him into the shelter.

Now, everyone knows Republicans and Democrats rarely see eye-to-eye. The divide has only grown deeper and wider since the 2016 Presidential election, and many congressmen won't even speak to each other now. But, miraculously, the minute players on the Democrat's team heard about the shooting of their compatriot, they immediately huddled together to pray. All told, sixteen Democrats set aside their differences to lift Scalise and others who were injured up in prayer.

Someone took a picture that morning, and it shows normally buttoned-up politicians, now wearing shorts and T-shirts, with their arms wrapped around each other and their heads bowed in prayer. I wish that picture could be displayed every time someone says it's impossible for the two political parties to get along; or that it's too hard to pray for people who have offended us.

In the end, whether we're asked to pray for a friend or foe, the Bible tells us our response should be the same. We should recognize it's not just our right, but our privilege, to go to the Lord on the person's behalf.

You have heard that it was said, 'Love your neighbor and hate your enemy.' But I tell you, love your enemies and pray for those who persecute you, that you may be children of your Father in heaven...[6]

---

[6] Matthew 5:43-45, NIV

Later, Paul wrote to the people of Philippi, which was a city in ancient Greece, and said basically the same thing: it's a Christian's duty to lift others up in prayer. Not just when it's convenient, or we're the only one who's available, or it happens to be someone we like.

Don't worry about anything: instead, pray about everything. Tell God what you need and thank him for all he has done. [7]

Paul had his share of challenges and life-threatening episodes with authorities, so he knew better than anyone else how important it was to pray. It's something to remember the next time we find ourselves asking "Who me?" whenever we're faced with a new prayer request.

---

[7] Philippians 4:6, NLT

What reasons do I have for putting off a prayer request?

____
____
____
____
____
____

What will it take to change my heart?

____
____
____
____
____
____

How can God use my reluctance for his glory?

____
____
____
____
____
____

though, once the chief finished praying. Why didn't the villagers storm the Paton's house that night and kill them?

It was quite simple; the chief was said to have replied. They were afraid of the army of men who surrounded the mission. Men with their swords drawn, who stood watch over the missionaries, although John knew no one had come to help them. No one, that is, but God's angels, who protected the couple as they prayed on the other side of the wall.

Reverend James Paton, John's brother, even wrote a book with his sibling called *The Story of John G. Patton, Thirty Years Among South Sea Cannibals*[9]. In it, the brothers detailed several accounts where the Paton's home was surrounded by villagers who wanted to kill them. Each time, the couple fell to their knees to pray, and each time, God saved them.

Examples of shameless persistence abound throughout the Bible. Like the Patons, another example comes to us courtesy of Elijah, the Old Testament prophet.

Roughly eight-hundred and fifty years before the birth of Christ, God sent Elijah to deliver some bad news to the king of Israel. God planned to turn off the water supply from heaven and plunge the people into a years-long drought, all because of the king's sinfulness. King Ahab worshipped idols, and he'd even built an altar to his favorite one, called Baal.

Now, no king wants to be told God took notice of his sinful ways and planned to punish his people for it. In a classic case of blaming the messenger for the message, the king focused his anger on Elijah. God warned Elijah the king planned to harm him, and he told the prophet to run far away, to the seaside town of Zarephath.

What happened there confused Elijah, though. God provided him with shelter through a poor widow who had nothing to her name but a child. The widow took Elijah in, and in return, God provided the family with food while the rest of the country starved. Then, inexplicably, the child became sick and died, which didn't bode well for Elijah, since he was supposed to help the family as a thank-you for the widow's

---

[9] Originally published January 1889

willingness to take him in. In 1 Kings 17 we read:

Sometime later, the woman's son became sick. He grew worse and worse, and finally he died. Then she (the widow) said to Elijah, "Oh man of God, what have you done to me? Have you come here to point out my sins and kill my son?"

But Elijah replied, "Give me your son." And he took the child's body from her arms, carried him up the stairs to the room where he was staying, and laid the body on his bed. Then Elijah cried out to the Lord, "O Lord my God, why have you brought tragedy to this widow who has opened her home to me, causing her son to die?"

And he stretched himself out over the child three times and cried out to the Lord, "O Lord my God, please let this child's life return to him." The Lord heard Elijah's prayer, and the life of the child returned, and he revived. Then Elijah brought him down from the upper room and gave him to his mother. "Look!" he said. "Your son is alive!" [10]

Some scholars believe Elijah had been in the family's house a whole year before the boy became ill. Since the child lingered for a while, perhaps Elijah prayed over him night after night, with no sign from God that he'd even heard the prayers.

How embarrassing. Here Elijah was a man of God, and he couldn't help the child of his host.

But then we get to the good part. After the boy died, Elijah took the child up to his own room and prayed over him. Not once, not twice, but three times. Each time, he cried out to God to breathe life back into the boy. And each time, he threw himself across the child, which meant he was all-in—physically, mentally and spiritually—when it came to the child's healing.

For those of you who've studied the passage, did you ever wonder why Elijah cried out three times? Why didn't he just pray once, and then sit back on his heels and wait for God's response?

Maybe he did pause after the first time. We'll never know if

---

[10] I Kings 17:17-23, NLT

he waited just long enough for God to work a miracle, and seeing none, he decided to try again. The point is that he didn't give up, even though he had irrefutable proof nothing had changed with the child. The boy remained dead after Elijah first approached God; his mother continued to wail one floor below them; and Elijah had a credibility problem on his hands.

Whenever I pray now, I try to remember Elijah and his wholehearted fight for the widow's son.

Another great example of someone who fought with prayer comes to us from a famous politician: Edward M. Kennedy. In 2002, Senator Kennedy's oldest child, Kara, was diagnosed with inoperable lung cancer. Doctors predicted she only had a year to live.

Kara was Kennedy's only daughter, born two years before he entered the Senate. In his 2009 memoir, *True Compass*, he wrote that he had "never seen a more beautiful baby, nor been happier in my life."

Of course, he was devasted when he was told about Kara's cancer. His daughter had two young children at home, a busy schedule of volunteer work, and a career as a documentary filmmaker. Why would God allow cancer to invade his only daughter's body?

Instead of railing against the unfairness of it all, or becoming despondent, Senator Kennedy took a different tack. He began to visit a Boston cathedral —the Basilica of Our Lady of Perpetual Hope—every day to pray for his daughter's healing. Every day.

Now, U.S. Senators have extremely busy schedules, full of meetings with constituents and dignitaries; multiple committee assignments; political fundraisers; interviews with the media; and on and on. It's enough to make someone's head spin. And, since Senator Kennedy had served in the Senate for four decades already, everyone in politics knew him, and he knew them. Which meant everyone wanted a moment of his time.

Instead of giving in to the demands of such a high-profile career, Senator Kennedy chose to put everything aside to pray for his daughter. Daily. He'd slip into the cathedral unnoticed, light a candle for her healing, and then he'd disappear again. A year later, doctors at Brigham and

Women's Hospital in Boston removed part of Kara's right lung, and she was declared cancer-free.

I can only imagine how many people tried to discourage Senator Kennedy from "wasting" his time when he went away to pray. How many aides tried to talk him into going to another meeting instead, or taking another call, or visiting with a wealthy fundraiser? But Senator Kennedy understood something a lot of people don't: he was in a fight for Kara's life, and he was prepared to beseech God with shameless persistence until her condition changed.

In writing this book, I came across a verse that startled me at first, because I'd never thought about it when I considered prayer. Not only are we to fight for others with prayer, and do with so with shameless persistence, but we are supposed to banish doubt beforehand.

In James 1:6, the author writes:

He must ask in faith without any doubting, for the one who doubts is like the surf of the sea, driven and tossed by the wind.[11]

Here James is specifically talking about why we shouldn't doubt when we ask God for wisdom; or we want to know what he would have us do in a particular situation.

Now, I was raised with the idea I should have faith "like a mustard seed,"[12] but I never thought about the role doubt could play in prayer. It reminds of when my children asked me for something they didn't really expect to receive. They'd giggle afterward, or squirm while they asked, because they knew I probably wouldn't say yes.

If we're like that with God, and we don't really expect to receive what we're asking for, why should he grant the request? James even writes:

Such people should not expect to receive anything from

---

[11] James 1:6, New American Standard Bible (NASB)

[12] Matthew 17:20, King James Version (KJV)

the Lord. [13]

It's as if we predetermine the answer when we don't place our trust in God.

In the end, I want to approach my prayer time like Senator Kennedy, the prophet Elijah, or missionaries John and Mary Patton did. All in. Willing to fight for someone or something until the very end. Confident God will answer the request, no matter what that answer might be.

Are you willing to do that, too?

---

[13] James 1:7, NLT

What's stopping me from going "all in" during my prayer time?

____

____

____

____

Is there something I've stopped praying for because I don't think God will ever grant it?

____

____

____

____

What will it take for me to boldly bring my secret desires to God?

____

____

____

____

Chapter 6: CONSIDER THE WATCHKEEPER

Of all the things we consider when we pray, the *where* of it probably doesn't figure into the equation. Why should we care about *where* we pray, when it's the *what* that counts?

After all, isn't prayer's portability what makes it so wonderful? We can pray anytime, anywhere, from the driver's seat of a car sitting in rush-hour traffic to a metal desk in a homeroom or a hardbacked chair in a chilly ICU waiting room.

Of course, sometimes people don't have a choice about where they pray. When the Apostle Paul was imprisoned in Caesarea, he was forced to ignore the sounds of the jail around him when he prayed. He probably heard everything from the rattle of chains to shouts amongst the guards and wails from people tired of being imprisoned.

Unlike Paul, though, we usually *do* have a choice of where we pray. Which brings us to the watchkeeper. If anyone understands the importance of location, location, location (besides Realtors), it's someone who works on a ship. Cargo barges, cruise ships, navy battleships and all sorts of sailing vessels employ someone (or a few people) to work as "watchkeeper" onboard.

While it sounds like the watchkeeper's job is to check the time, it's actually his or her job to be constantly on the lookout for obstacles that could sink the ship. This person stands on deck and scans the horizon behind a pair of high-powered binoculars, or she takes up a position in the bridge, so she can eye a bank of radar screens.

The goal is to avoid obstacles at all costs. What does this have to do with prayer?

Everything. It illustrates the importance of guarding against obstacles that could derail our prayer time. Obstacles that could sabotage our best efforts, if we're not careful.

Maybe your obstacle is a new puppy that needs constant potty breaks. Or, the seductive blue glow of a computer screen on the desk in your home office. Maybe it's the constant ping of a cell phone that alerts you to new messages. All those seemingly innocent things can get in the way of morning (or nighttime) prayers and upend even the most-sincere efforts to stay on track.

When the movie "The War Room" debuted in 2015, few people probably realized the idea of praying in a closet was borrowed from someone who lived more than three-hundred years ago. John Wesley, one of the men who founded the Methodist church, was well-known for praying in a closet he built next to his bedroom.

Just like in the movie, Wesley kept his prayer room free of distractions. He placed a Bible, a footstool and a bookstand there; but not much else. Wesley would rise every day at four o'clock in the morning and shuffle from his bedroom to this closet, where he would pray for two hours at a time.

It was here that Wesley developed his landmark ideas about how to organize a church, and where he prayed for the lay pastors he ordained. People say he got the idea for the prayer closet from his mother, who raised ten children in a raucous household. Susanna Wesley shut herself off from her clamoring brood by throwing her apron over her head in the middle of her kitchen. The tent she fashioned warned her children not to interrupt her, because she was deep in prayer.

Truth be told, distractions are often Satan's way of disturbing your prayer time. Because his goal is to drag us further from God, not bring us closer, he'll do everything in his power to interrupt the time we spend with our Maker.

The Apostle Peter learned this lesson the hard way in the book of Matthew. Soon after Jesus fed the five thousand, he sent the crowds away so he could pray in private. Meanwhile, Peter and his cohorts settled into the hull of a boat to catch some much-needed shut-eye. At one point, a nasty windstorm arose.

Jesus walked across the surface of Lake Tiberius, better known as the Sea of Galilee, to reach the disciples as they thrashed about in the boat. Only Peter was brave enough to call out for Christ's help:

Then Peter called to him, "Lord, if it's really you, tell me to come to you, walking on the water."

"Yes, come," Jesus said.

So Peter went over the side of the boat and walked on the water toward Jesus.[14]

I don't know about you, but I like to think I would've been so enchanted with the miracle taking place beneath my feet that I'd lock eyes on my savior and never waver. Maybe that's what Peter thought, too. Until he noticed the whitecaps whipping all around him. Saw the sea spray funneling up like miniature tornadoes. Heard the sickening sound of water sloshing over the side of the boat. At that moment, Peter became distracted by all the "stuff" happening around him, and that's when he lost his footing.

But when he saw the strong wind and the waves, he was terrified and began to sink. "Save me, Lord!" he shouted.[15]

What might've happened if Peter stayed focused on the task at hand? If he kept his eyes trained on Jesus, instead of letting everything else cloud his concentration? He could've spared himself a frigid dunk in the lake, for one thing.

But perhaps the best words of wisdom about the "where" of prayer belong to Jesus. He often traveled to a mountaintop or another secluded area when he needed to be alone with his Father.

He went off by himself when it was time to choose his twelve apostles, for example. [16] He knew it was a critical decision, because his time on earth was short and these men would take over his ministry.

He also sequestered himself after feeding that crowd with loaves and fishes, right before Peter got dunked in the waves:

After sending them home, he went up into the hills by

---

[14] Matthew 14:28-29, NLT

[15] Matthew 14:30, NLT

[16] Luke 6:12, NLT

himself to pray. Night fell while he was there alone. [17]

As if those personal examples weren't enough, Jesus spelled it out for us when he said:

But when you pray, go away by yourself, shut the door behind you, and pray to your Father in private. Then your Father, who sees everything, will reward you. [18]

Remember the story about Elijah and the widow's son from Chapter 5? He could've made a big production out of praying for the child by prostrating himself in the middle of the woman's living room. While that might've impressed his host, and even given Elijah an "out" if God didn't grant the request ("See? I did my best") that's not what he did. He chose to pray for the child in private; somewhere he wouldn't be disturbed:

...And he took the child's body from her arms, carried him up to the room where he was staying, and laid the body on his bed.[19]

Someone else who faced an overwhelming number of distractions—and learned to put them aside— was Mother Teresa. When the iconic saint from Macedonia won a Nobel Peace Prize in 1979, she became a worldwide celebrity. Everyone wanted to interview her, or visit her, or tour the place where she carried out her ministry. While it was a boon for the Missionaries of Charity, her organization, it easily could've upended her schedule.

Only that didn't happen. Mother Teresa remained committed to keeping the same prayer schedule she always did: with hour-long blocks booked aside each day. Why? Here she says it in her own words:

---

[17] Matthew 14:23, NLT

[18] Matthew 6:6, NLT

[19] I Kings 17:19, NLT

"I make a Holy Hour each day in the presence of Jesus in the Blessed Sacrament. All my sisters of the Missionaries of Charity make a daily Holy Hour as well, because we find that through our daily Holy Hour our love for Jesus becomes more intimate, our love for each other more understanding, and our love for the poor more compassionate."[20]

During the Holy Hour, Catholics spend the time contemplating how Jesus suffered in the Garden of Gethsemane. It's based on the book of Matthew, when Jesus asked his disciples to keep him company while he prayed:

(1) *Then he said to them, "My soul is overwhelmed with sorrow to the point of death. Stay here and keep watch with me."*
(2) *Going a little farther, he fell with his face to the ground and prayed, "My Father, if it is possible, may this cup be taken from me. Yet not as I will, but as you will." Then he returned to his disciples and found them sleeping. "Couldn't you men keep watch with me for one hour?" he asked Peter.*[21]

Mother Teresa not only spent an hour herself on the practice, but she instituted it into the daily schedule for the sisters from the Missionaries of Charity. That's how much she believed in communing with God at a set time each day.

Do you have a hidden corner of your house, where you can hide away from the hungry puppy, or a talkative spouse, or the thousand-and-one chores that need finishing? How about an office stairwell at work? What about a light-filled corner of your living room?

Before you designate a certain spot for prayer, consider the work of a researcher who studied the role of the

---

[20] *Mother Teresa on Perpetual Adoration*. Retrieved from: https://www.stmatthew.net/faqs-new-perpetual-adoration-chapel.

[21] Matthew 26:38-40, NIV

environment on our thoughts.

This researcher, a professor at the University of Minnesota, looked at how things like colors, light, and even ceiling height affect us when we contemplate something.[22]

For one thing, she found people tended to think big-picture thoughts when they sat in a room with a high ceiling. She said people who had a major decision to make, or wanted to contemplate their futures, should do it without being boxed in by a low ceiling. Conversely, she found that people who needed to focus on specifics, say an upcoming geometry test or a meeting with a client, did better when sitting in a low-ceilinged room, free of distractions.

While John Wesley seemed to do just fine sitting in a four-foot by six-foot closet, it's something to think about when we approach the "where" of our prayer time. Although God will listen to our prayers whether they come from a storeroom, a jail cell, or a battlefield bunker, it's for our benefit that we create the most intimate, distraction-free space possible.

Here's a final story about the power of place when it comes to our prayers.

According to *Catholic Digest,* which shared the story in its online journal in 2018, Crossroads Correctional Center is a maximum-security prison in Missouri. Each week, a priest would conduct a gathering for inmates who wanted to partake in communion.

Now, prisons are anything but warm and welcoming. So, the inmates gathered in a nondescript breakroom, where the only thing they had to focus on was four white walls.

Normally, the priest performed the rites on Wednesdays, but that all changed when a local teenager was involved in a horrible car crash. The situation was so bleak, the priest told the prisoners, the boy's family was told to prepare his funeral.

So, each week the twelve inmates gathered in that breakroom, only now they prayed over the teenager, fervently

---

[22] Joan Meyers-Levy, *Journal of Consumer Research*, Volume 34, Issue 2, August 2007, Pages 174–186.

asking God to heal him. And each week, despite the doctors' predictions, the boy recovered a little bit more. After the inmates had prayed for him for many months, the hospital finally discharged the teen.

The priest, Father Phil Luebbert, said he believed the prayers of those twelve inmates, spoken in that bleak, nondescript prison breakroom, made all the difference in the world.

In the end, while *what* we pray is more important than *where* we pray, it's something to think about. Even though God doesn't care whether we pray in a perfectly appointed library, surrounded by classic books and costly furniture, or in a closet made of plywood and paste, it's for our benefit we find a place that quiets our minds and stills our thoughts.

What are some of the obstacles I face during my prayer time?

____

____

____

____

____

____

How can I remove the obstacles to improve my concentration?

____

____

____

____

____

____

In a perfect world, where would I pray and why?

____

____

____

____

____

____

Chapter 7: THE AFTERMATH OF YES

Once God says yes to a prayer request, everything else should fall into place, right? We should bound out of bed every morning full of praise and worship for the one who orchestrated our recovery/new job/repaired marriage, etc. (We should start every day that way, even when God says no, but that's a subject for another chapter.)

That's how it was for me when I first got home from the hospital. I wanted to shout from the mountaintops that God had healed me. Since Houston doesn't have hills, let alone mountains, I would've settled for a nearby water tower.

My euphoria lasted several weeks. Whenever someone new asked about my recovery, I didn't hesitate to give God the credit. I would state without a doubt that he, and he alone, was responsible for my healing. A simple question of "How are you?" could lead to a ten-minute monologue on how fortunate I was God had chosen to spare my life. (My apologies to anyone I overwhelmed during those first few days and weeks!)

Then a funny thing happened. Although, I don't consider it funny anymore, since I've come to realize it was a ploy by Satan to destroy my perspective. After a few weeks of readily testifying to God's part in my healing, a tiny doubt wiggled its way into the spaces of my heart.

What if it wasn't really God who healed me, but the medicine doctors continually pumped into my veins? Modern medicine is a wonderful thing, after all, and we're now living in the greatest age of medical discovery the world has ever known.

If not the medicine, maybe it was the brilliant physicians who healed me. These men and women graduated from places like Duke University Medical School, where only seven percent of all applicants are accepted. Maybe it was their smarts that made the difference.

(Do you see the irony there? Satan would love for me to give credit for my healing to the humans who treated me, instead of the God who created those humans in the first place.)

Finally, I marveled at the technology that surrounded me in the hospital. Everything from MRI machines that cost thousands of dollars, if not more, to high-powered scopes that are no thicker than a pencil. And what about those newfangled diagnostic tests that give doctors results in thirty minutes or less? Maybe it was the machines, or the tests, or the procedures that changed the outcome for me.

There's only one problem with that line of thinking, though: even my doctors didn't expect me to live. Here I had all the right medicine, all the up-to-date procedures, and a hospital full of whiz-bang technology, and no one knew how to save me. Plus, other patients have had access to those very same things, but their stories have turned out much differently.

I can't be the only one who's done this. Who's questioned whether God was the one to answer the prayer, or whether the change came from happenstance. Maybe you've seen a break in your spouse's bad behavior—something you've long prayed for—but when it finally comes, you chalk it up to those expensive counseling sessions you went through. The money that suddenly appeared when you so desperately needed it? Just a coincidence, you tell yourself. Payback from the universe for all those times you've helped someone else.

Even winning a job can be explained away by giving credit to your recruiter, your background, the timing. See? It's easy to think-away God's miracles or blessings, and to give the credit to someone other than him.

"Blessing amnesia" isn't the only thing that can happen after God says yes to a prayer request. Sometimes, it makes us want to ask for more. Let's call this the "more, please," response to our answered prayer.

"The unexpected money was nice," we might pray, "but not quite the windfall that would solve all my problems. Could you maybe add a few zeros next time, God?"

Or, we could thank him for giving us that job, but then we change our tune once we're actually doing the work. Then, we'll complain about the long commute, or the small paycheck, or the monotony of it all. And we'll have the audacity to turn around and pray for a promotion…or a raise…or the chance to work from home. We'll do anything but focus on the here-and-now of the gift he's given us.

This isn't a new problem. It happened to the Israelites, too, once they followed Moses out of Egypt and wandered into the wilderness. God provided them with manna (which the writer of Psalm 78 called the "bread of heaven"[23]) and it gave every family the exact amount they needed to make it through a day.

Instead of praising God for this blessing, though, the Israelites soon became picky. It wasn't enough God had miraculously provided them with food from heaven; now they wanted a say in the menu.

"…Oh, for some meat," they exclaimed. "We remember the fish we used to eat for free in Egypt. And we had all the cucumbers, melons, leeks, onions, and garlic we wanted. But now our appetites are gone. All we ever see is this manna!"[24]

If it was me the Israelites were appealing to, I'd have rolled my eyes right about then. Here God gave them what they needed, in an incredible display of his power, but they still wanted more.

"Blessing amnesia" and the "more, please" attitude is such a human response to God's gifts. It happened all the time in the Bible, even when people came face to face with the one who was responsible for their answered prayer.

More than fifteen-hundred years after the Israelites complained about their diet, Jesus was traveling to Jerusalem for a final time with his disciples. They came across some lepers who were forced to stand apart from everyone else.

Now it happened as He went to Jerusalem that He passed through the midst of Samaria and Galilee. Then as He entered a certain village, there met Him ten men who were lepers, who stood afar off. And they lifted up their voices, and said, "Jesus, Master, have mercy on us!" So when He saw them, He said to

---

[23] Psalms 78:24, NLT

[24] Numbers 11:4-6, NLT

them, "Go, show yourselves to the priests." And so, it was that as they went, they were cleansed. And one of them, when he saw that he was healed, returned, and with a loud voice glorified God, and fell down on his face at His feet, giving Him thanks. And he was a Samaritan. So Jesus answered and said, "Were there not ten cleansed? But where are the nine? Were there not any found who returned to give glory to God except this foreigner?" And He said to him, "Arise, go your way. Your faith has made you well."[25]

Even with irrefutable proof Jesus had healed them, ninety percent of the lepers never returned to give him thanks. It's as if they forgot he even existed once they had what they wanted. If that's not a lack of gratitude, I don't know what is.

Finally, I've noticed one more stumbling block when it comes to answered prayer: pride. It gets in the way of our seeing God's power for what it really is, while it tries to elevate ours.

Maybe, we think, God answered our prayer because of something we did. Maybe it's payback for all the times we worked in vacation Bible school, or supported our church's building campaign, or maybe we're just really, really good at saying the right things when we pray.

Hardly. Even though there are instances in the Bible when God granted someone's prayer request because of his or her faithfulness (Hezekiah comes to mind)[26], I don't think our righteousness alone determines whether God says yes to our prayers or not. If it did, only the very righteous would get a positive response, which we know isn't always the case.

An excellent example of someone who let pride ruin his relationship with God was Uzziah, the man who became king of Israel at the tender age of sixteen. He ruled over the Israelites for fifty-two years and God blessed him in every way imaginable. He never failed to give God credit for his success:

---

[25] Luke 17:11-19, New King James Version (NKJV)

[26] 2 Kings 20:3-5, NLT

And he did what was right in the sight of the Lord…[27]

But then pride reared its ugly head. Only twelve verses later, we read about Uzziah's downfall:

But when he had become powerful, he also became proud, which led to his downfall. He sinned against the Lord his God by entering the sanctuary of the Lord's temple and personally burning incense on the incense altar.[28]

Big mistake. That was the job for the high priest, not the king. When the high priest brought eighty of his associates and tried to convince Uzziah he'd sinned, the king became enraged. The story ends with Uzziah being struck with leprosy and living out his days as a hermit, excluded from the very people and place he once ruled over.

When God says yes, the result can be overwhelming joy, a dive into selfish pride, or an attitude of skepticism. Sometimes, it's a mix of all three.

How refreshing it is to hear about times God said yes so conclusively the outcome can't be explained away, or attributed to one's own goodness, or anything else but a flat-out miracle. I'll close this chapter with a yes God granted to a famous writer who sped from a war zone as a young correspondent.

Frederick Forsyth, who wrote such famous books as *The Day of the Jackal* and *The Odessa File*, spoke with *The Spectator* magazine when it asked for people's stories of modern-day miracles. [29]

---

[27] 2 Chronicles 26:4, NKJV

[28] 2 Chronicles 26:16, NLT

[29] The editors (2016, December). *Answered Prayers by Justin Welby and Others, The Spectator.*

Retrieved from: https://www.spectator.co.uk/2016/12/answered-prayers-by-justin-welby-amber-rudd-james-dyson-and-12-others/

Before he was a famous writer, Forsyth was a journalist for the *Daily Express* in England. He covered the Nigerian Civil War for that newspaper. Toward the war's end in 1970, he caught one of the last planes out of Biafra, which was a state in southeastern Nigeria that sought to be independent but failed.

Forsyth said the plane was an old DC-4 filled with dying children and Irish nuns. Here is the way he remembered the incident:

We struggled on three engines towards the ocean. After turning east towards Gabon, the starboard outer began to cough and splutter. It was clear the old rust-bucket would never fly on two and was sinking towards the sea on three.

He goes on to say he quietly prayed for a miracle and was astonished at what happened next:

Fortunately, the French had built Libreville airport close to the shore. The dangling wheels almost clipped the sand dunes, then we were over concrete. At that moment the coughing, spluttering engine gave up the ghost and the crippled aircraft dropped on to the tarmac.

An aging plane carrying too much weight had blown an engine over the ocean. Not exactly the ideal situation for a pilot to make an emergency landing. Yet, it happened. And an internationally recognized figure had to admit there was no other reason for that safe landing but prayer.

In the end, we need to remember that when God says yes, it doesn't mean we deserved the gift, or that we're better than others, or that God is one enormous Santa Claus we can return to whenever we want to ask for more. We should be watchful for pride, dissatisfaction and forgetfulness, and try to root them out whenever they appear. Fortunately for us, God still loves us, even when we don't handle the aftereffects of his answers very well:

...He is kind to the ungrateful and wicked.[30]

---

[30] Luke 6:35, NIV

When was the last time I tried to “explain away” something God did for me?

____
____
____
____

Do I ever catch myself taking credit for something God has done?

____
____
____
____

What will it take for me to be satisfied with God’s answers, and not look for “more, please?”

____
____
____
____

Chapter 8: WHY "WAIT" ISN'T A FOUR-LETTER WORD

After the birth of our oldest daughter, my husband and I waited two years before we decided to try for baby number two. We realized it might take a while for us to get pregnant, since we were both in our mid-thirties, but we were willing to wait. (Or, so we thought.)

One year passed, and then another. It got to the point where I automatically flinched whenever I handed over yet another home pregnancy test to the drugstore's cashier.

By now, my prayers had become a little more urgent, and a lot less patient. They even devolved into bargaining sessions, where I promised to give God anything in return for a positive pregnancy test. (As if he needed anything from me!)

In the meantime, my friends kept having baby showers, and I kept plastering a fake smile on my face and attending them. All those baby-girl-pink and little-boy-blue decorations! Cupcakes shaped like bassinets! Not to mention sweet, knitted booties and doll-sized cardigans. I couldn't help but ask God why he blessed so many people around me with more children, when he ignored (or so I thought) my request for the very same thing.

When another two years passed, and I still found myself in the checkout line at Walgreens paying for home pregnancy tests, we decided to take matters into our own hands. We visited a well-known fertility doctor here in Houston, certain he'd uncover the source of our problem and—ta da! —our little family of three would blossom to four.

We jumped headfirst into the strange world of infertility treatment. If you've ever been there, you know the hallmarks: complicated tests with names no one can pronounce; calendars for this, that and every other thing; medicines that cost a couple hundred dollars a pop.

Our infertility doctor was relentlessly upbeat about our chances for another child, though. He even met us at his locked offices one Sunday morning for a procedure that couldn't wait until after the weekend.

But, after a half-dozen procedures and several surgeries failed, even the enthusiasm of our infertility doctor flagged. Now the outcome was far from certain. And so, my prayers changed, yet again. I promised to never, ever ask God for another thing if he'd grant me this one, small favor. I'm sure my prayers sounded mildly hysterical by this point, and the farthest thing from grateful for everything I already had.

By the end of 1998, after we'd suffered through yet another failed in-vitro fertilization procedure, we threw in the towel. We were tired of spending so much money and tired of so much disappointment. We contacted a well-known adoption agency in Dallas and signed the papers to start the process. We even wrote a check for the deposit (unfortunately, private adoptions can cost as much as the down payment for a house), but my husband forgot to mail the check, so it sat for a few days on the edge of his desk.

What happened next was exquisite in that wonderful way God has of showing us who's really in charge. Remember that by this time, even our eternally optimistic infertility doctor advised us to stop trying for another biological child. So, imagine my shock when I found a leftover pregnancy test and decided to give it a whirl, rather than throw it away. You can guess what happened next: the test came back positive, my five-year-old daughter twirled around the living room, and there was much dancing and singing in our house that day.

The story doesn't end there, though. Not only did God grant the request of his impatient and ungrateful child (me), he orchestrated one final miracle. The Saturday morning I went into labor, my normal obstetrician wasn't available to oversee the delivery. Instead, the hospital assigned the doctor on call to be my physician. Sure enough…our infertility doctor waltzed through the doors of the delivery room and helped us welcome a second child into the world.

My daughter's birth taught me so many lessons. Lessons about gratitude (for the one child he'd already blessed us with, among other things), and lessons about grace (even though we questioned God's goodness, he still said yes to our prayer).

Now, when I look at our daughter Dana, I can't help but see a living, breathing reminder of God's faithfulness. In fact,

Dana was the one who drove me to the emergency room when I fell ill, which I believe was God's way of bringing our family's story around full circle.

Countless people have waited weeks, months, or even years for an answer to their prayers, like my family did. Way back in I Samuel, the prophet tells us the story of David. Now, David was supposed to be anointed the next king of Israel, since King Saul had failed so miserably at the job. In I Samuel 16:13 we read:

So, as David stood there among his brothers, Samuel took the flask of olive oil he had brought and anointed David with the oil.[31]

Not bad for the runt of a litter (David) whose own father didn't consider him a candidate for the top job when Samuel asked to see his sons. After Samuel proclaimed David would be the next king, the teenager enjoyed even more success: he felled a giant in the Valley of Elah with just a slingshot and a river rock.

Life couldn't be better for David. Crowds adored him, women sang songs about him, and he'd finally earned the respect of his father and brothers. Basically, he was a rock star in Israel, which enraged King Saul even more.

So, Saul decided to snuff out his rival for good, and David fled to the hills of Adullam. The land actually lies some two miles south of where David felled the giant, so it's quite possible the teenager could view the site of his greatest success on the way to his brand-new home: a dank, dark cave.

For several years, David hid in those caves, accompanied by a troop of four-hundred misfits who decided they'd rather live there than submit to the rule of Saul. Here, David was supposed to take over the reins as king of Israel, and instead, he slept, ate and worked with his motley crew in a burrow better suited to a mountain gazelle than a troop of men.

Anyone would expect David to be bitter at this point. Not to

---

[31] I Samuel 16:13, NLT

mention hurt, disappointed and angry. Instead, we see how he reacted to God's plan:

My heart is confident in you, oh God; my heart is confident. No wonder I can sing your praises![32]

David wrote those words in the midst of one of his greatest disappointments. But the wait wasn't in vain. Imagine how much David learned from his roommates about what *not* to do when he finally became their king. God was preparing David for the role of a lifetime during those bleak years, when things looked their worst.

The Bible is filled with versus for people who are in the midst of waiting:

But they who wait for the Lord shall renew their strength; they shall mount up with wings like eagles; they shall run and not be weary; they shall walk and not faint.[33]

More than that, we rejoice in our sufferings, knowing that suffering produces endurance, and endurance produces character, and character produces hope. [34]

Of course, we don't always feel like Paul did —hopeful— when we're waiting. More often than not, we feel forgotten by God, and we wonder if he'll ever answer us.

If anyone knew that feeling, it was Ruth Graham, the wife of famous evangelist Billy Graham. I don't know about you, but I've always thought the Graham family was above reproach. Surely, they had their own private telephone line to heaven, so they could talk to God twenty-four/seven.

But even the Grahams weren't immune to family conflict.

---

[32] Psalm 57:7, NLT

[33] Isaiah 40:31, English Standard Version (ESV)

[34] Romans 5:3-4, ESV

The couple's fourth and fifth children were self-described "partiers." In fact, Franklin, the fourth, was sent to a Christian boarding school while a teenager, only to drop out. Then, when his parents enrolled him at LeTourneau University in Longview, Texas, he was expelled for breaking the rules.

Ouch! Can you imagine how that phone call went? I wouldn't want to be the person who had to tell the world-famous evangelist his son was being expelled from college. Talk about awkward! And all that time, Franklin's mother quietly prayed her son would come to his senses.

Once, when she was traveling far from home, Graham said she was awakened in the middle of the night by troubling thoughts about her kids. So, she turned to Philippians 4:

Do not be anxious about anything, but in everything by prayer and supplication with thanksgiving let your requests be made known to God. And the peace of God, which surpasses all understanding, will guard your hearts and your minds in Christ Jesus.[35]

The result? Here it is in her own words:

Suddenly I realized the missing ingredient in my prayers had been "with thanksgiving." So, I put down my Bible and spent time worshiping Him for who and what He is. [36]

It took many years for the Graham boys to finally get their acts together, but Ruth lived to see her prayers answered. Franklin went on to take over his father's worldwide ministry, while Ned ultimately headed up East Gate Ministries, which publishes Bibles in China.

What might've happened if Ruth gave up on her rebellious children and focused on something else instead? Heaven only knows she had a lot on her plate, with three other children to worry about, a world-famous husband, and her own ministry in

---

[35] Philippians 4:6-7, NIV

[36] Graham, Ruth Bell. *It's My Turn.* (Fleming H. Revell Co., 1982).

the works. At some point, I wonder if she ever lost hope.

In one of her other books, this one titled *Letters from Ruth's Attic*, she wrote:

The Christian life is like climbing a mountain. For some people, the climb is a gently sloping ascent; for other people, the climb is like attacking the north face of the Eiger.[37]

Maybe praying for those rebellious sons felt to Ruth like climbing a mountain. If so, she never stopped climbing, and she continued to pray for her boys, even when all seemed hopeless.

Here's the point: whenever we hike up a mountainside, we don't get to see what's on the other side. We never get to glimpse the easy-going, downward slope. All we see is the craggy face of the rock in front of us, and maybe a path littered with debris by our side. It can be discouraging, yes. But it also can be encouraging to learn about people, like Ruth Graham, who climbed their own mountains and ultimately made it to the other side.

The same could be said of Martin Luther King, Jr., the famous civil rights leader. Whenever I think of Dr. King, I think of someone who changed our country's political landscape seemingly overnight. In reality, Dr. King had to wait many years to see his dream of an integrated America become reality. And then, he only got to enjoy it for a few short years before he was assassinated.

As schoolchildren, we all learned the basics about Dr. King's life: he was ordained as a minister; he focused his work in Alabama, which was ground zero for the civil rights movement; and he tragically died at the age of thirty-nine.

But did you know Dr. King's first major demonstration—the Montgomery, Alabama, bus boycott in 1955—lasted almost a full year before the Supreme Court ruled against segregation on public busses?

Before then, bus lines never hired African-Americans to be

---

[37] Graham, Ruth Bell. *Letters From Ruth's Attic*. (Billy Graham Evangelistic Association, 2015).

drivers; they let only Caucasians sit at the front of the bus; and African-Americans often had to give up their seats to their light-skinned neighbors.

During the three-hundred-and-eighty-two-day boycott, Dr. King's house was firebombed, he was arrested, and he subsequently spent two weeks in jail. It wasn't until the end of December, 1956, that the Supreme Court's ruling went into effect, and African-Americans could finally sit where they wanted on a public bus.

And what happened next? During the years that followed, Dr. King continued to fight, to no avail. He marched; he traveled on behalf of the cause; he met with world leaders, including Dwight Eisenhower, John F. Kennedy and Malcolm X. He also wrote several books, including a compilation of his sermons and an account of the Montgomery bus strike called *Stride Toward Freedom: the Montgomery Story.*

But seven years after the bus boycott, Dr. King grew disappointed with the movement. He lamented the state of our country's civil rights, because he considered America to be far behind the rest of the world.

He wrote:

The nations of Asia and Africa are moving with jet-like speed toward gaining political independence, but we still creep at horse and buggy pace toward gaining a cup of coffee at a lunch counter.[38]

It took until 1964 for the Civil Rights Act to be passed, and with it, for real reform to come to America. That's nine years after the original bus protest started, and after countless hours of prayer by Dr. King and others.

No doubt God was using that time, though, for something very important: to groom Dr. King for an even greater challenge. Perhaps if Dr. King hadn't been arrested almost a dozen times overall (including once for tax fraud, for which he was exonerated); if he didn't endure physical violence, such

---

[38] King, Dr. Martin L. *Why We Can't Wait* (Harper & Row, 1964).

as being stabbed with a letter opener; if he didn't crisscross the country, gaining promise after promise, only to see those promises broken; maybe then he wouldn't have been so impassioned when he gave his famous "I Have A Dream" speech.

That iconic speech, given at the steps of the Lincoln Memorial in 1963, sparked the fire that became the roaring Civil Rights Act of 1964. All told, it happened almost ten years after the first bus boycott. Not exactly an overnight success, was it? But Dr. King no doubt cherished it all the more because so many hours, tears and prayer went into it.

We all realize, at some level, that we prize things even more if we have to wait for them. It's what we learn as children, when we pounce on our Christmas presents come December 25. Most kids spend days, or even weeks, gazing at tantalizing packages with pretty bows, practically salivating at the thought of what's inside them.

We all do it. Maybe it's not a Christmas present, but a new car in the showroom window of our local dealership that catches our eye. If only we could save enough money for the down payment, that car would be ours. Or, maybe it's the cute guy in accounting who can't quite work up the nerve to ask us out. When he does, the heavens sing.

Now, even scientists say it's not an "old-wives tale." They tell us research bears out what we've long suspected: waiting increases our enjoyment of something.

In a recent study, published in the *Journal of Consumer Research* [39], the authors measured the ways waiting impacts our enjoyment.

They asked participants at a Hong Kong university what they'd rather have: a small box of Godiva chocolates now, or a larger box later (after a month or so).

The people who chose to wait for the chocolates in the study gave it higher marks than people who got them right away. The "waiters" also said they'd be willing to pay more for

---

[39] D. Xianxhi, A. Fishbach, "How Nonconsumption Shapes Desire." (*Journal of Consumer Research*, Volume 41, Issue 4, 1 December 2014).

the chocolates than the people who didn't have to wait as long.

"When people wait, it makes them place a higher value on what they're waiting for," researcher Ayelet Fishbach scientifically concluded.

It's something to think about the next time you find yourself on "hold" when it comes to your prayers. Maybe God is using this time to prepare you for what's coming next, or he's causing you to realize how much—or how little—you really value what you're waiting for.

There's one last aspect to waiting that's rarely discussed. As humans, we have a way of tuning out what we don't want to hear.

Could it be that God has already answered your prayer, only you're less-than-thrilled with the answer?

It's the old "fingers-in-the-ears, la-la-la" trick kids know so well. If they ask for something from mom and dad, and they don't like the answer, they'll stuff their chubby little fingers in their ears and pretend they were never answered at all.

In a way, this was Gideon's response when God appeared to him in the form of an angel. The Israelites had received so many good things from God in the Old Testament—freedom from Egypt, a path out of the wilderness, and their ultimate arrival at the Promised Land—and what did they do? They blew it by creating idols and worshipping other gods.

So, God appeared to Gideon and told him he'd been chosen to free Israel from their oppressors, the Midianites. Instead of welcoming the news, Gideon basically turned on God and asked him why he hadn't answered their prayers yet:

"Pardon me, my lord," Gideon replied, "but if the Lord is with us, why has all this happened to us? Where are all his wonders that our ancestors told us about when they said, 'Did not the Lord bring us up out of Egypt?' But now the Lord has abandoned us and given us into the hand of Midian."[40]

Apparently, the Israelites didn't like what God had to say

---

[40] Judges 6:13, NLT

about their behavior, and instead, they grew disappointed when they thought God was ignoring their request.

God had clearly warned the Israelites they shouldn't adopt the idols of their captors, but they didn't listen to him. They went with the "waiting for an answer" ploy rather than turning away from their wicked ways.

In the end, God can use the time we spend waiting to prepare us for what comes next. It also gives us a chance to fully appreciate the object of our desire. And, finally, it may be that God's already answered our prayer, but we don't like the answer, and we're holding out hope for something different.

Do you fall into any of those camps? I know I have, and it gives me a new perspective on what to do when I feel like my prayer has been placed "on hold."

Is there a prayer I'm still waiting on?

____
____
____
____

Can anything good come from this time of waiting?

____
____
____
____

How can I use this time to glorify God…even when I don't feel like it?

____
____
____
____

Chapter 9: WHEN THE ANSWER IS NO

Nothing feels worse than praying wholeheartedly for something, only to be told no. Maybe you've prayed for a seriously ill child, or an elderly parent, or a marriage that's on the rocks, but the worst happens anyway.

About ten years after our struggle with infertility, I developed a horrible case of insomnia. I did everything right: I exercised; I cut caffeine from my diet; I maintained the same bedtime routine night after night. Nothing changed. I began to sleep only every-other-night, which meant I spent half my days bleary and miserable. It was a vicious cycle that left me exhausted, and it colored everything from our family life to my marriage.

Finally, I went to see a Christian counselor, who suggested I study the Bible during those sleepless hours and pray for God to heal my broken body clock.

Guess what? I followed his advice, but I still couldn't sleep. Night after night, I'd lie awake and wonder why God had abandoned me. Why would he let me suffer, when he supposedly loved me and wanted only the best for me? It sure didn't feel like the best when I muddled through my days with my brain in a perpetual fog.

When I finally did find relief, it didn't happen for many months, by which time I'd convinced myself I must be doing something wrong.

Now I can look back and see the point of that whole episode: I think God was trying to teach me something. He allowed me to suffer so I could develop empathy for others; which was something that didn't come naturally to me. He also was teaching me to rely on him and not on my own strength, when what I desperately wanted was to control my nights.

While my experience with insomnia can't compare to a parent who loses a child to cancer, or a husband who must bury a beloved spouse, or a family that faces financial ruin, it *did* give me a small insight into how horrible it can feel when

God says no.

Once I got out of the intensive care unit in early 2018, I often wondered why God chose to spare my life and say yes to the people who prayed over me. Why did he grant a yes in my case, but he's said no to so many others?

I'm not the only person who wondered about it. Several people approached me after my discharge and asked me why God would spare my life, and then take away the life of their family member or loved one. They didn't mean to be cruel; they just wanted to understand the difference between what happened to me and what happened to their beloved.

I still don't think it's a matter of righteousness. (See Chapter 5.) Many stalwart Christians have dedicated their entire lives to doing God's work, but they still die young, or they suffer another terrible fate.

No, I don't think my "goodness" was the reason I survived. I don't think I could ever be good enough or righteous enough or important enough to warrant that.

Whenever I wonder about the "why" of it, I'm reminded of Jesus' experience in the Garden of Gethsemane. Here was God's own son, on his knees, begging his Father to spare him from the cruel death that was about to come. Jesus prefaced his words with "If it is possible," [41] but the meaning was clear: Please save me from this fate. And what happened? God told him no. He allowed his own son to be crucified, in the most horrible way imaginable.

How much did God want to spare his son that day? More than we can ever know or understand. But it didn't change the outcome.

A thousand or so years earlier, King David experienced something similar when his own son fell ill.

David begged God to spare the child. He went without food and lay all night on the bare ground. The elders of his household pleaded with him to get up and eat with them, but he refused.[42]

---

[41] Matthew 26:39, NLT

[42] 2 Samuel 12:16-17, NIV

After seven days of this, the child died. Here was a man after God's own heart[43] and his very name meant "beloved." But none of that mattered when David asked God to spare his son.

It wasn't the only time God denied one of David's requests, either. It happened again when David later wanted to build a temple to honor God.

"...but God said to me, you must not build a temple to honor my name, for you are a warrior and have shed much blood."[44]

David provides just one example of what can happen to even the most beloved of God's children. About three-thousand years later, something similar happened to the writer and theologian C.S. Lewis.

Lewis wrote more than thirty books over his lifetime, including the *Chronicles of Narnia* series, which sold more than one-hundred-million copies worldwide. Once an atheist, he converted to Christianity at the age of thirty-three and wrote *The Pilgrim's Regress* a few years later to chronicle his religious journey.

He followed that up with such classics as *Mere Christianity* and *The Screwtape Letters*. If ever a person deserved a pass on hard times, it was Lewis. Countless people turned to Christ because of him, including the woman who would later become his wife.

Lewis married Joy Davidman in 1956, when he was almost sixty years old. They'd been friends for a decade, but they got to enjoy their marriage for only a short time. In 1957, Davidman officially was diagnosed with bone and breast cancer.

Lewis was devasted. When he heard about a priest who could supposedly heal people, he called for the man and

---

[43] 1 Samuel 13:14, NLT

[44] 1 Chronicles 28:3, NLT

asked him to pray over his wife. Davidman's cancer went into remission for a short time, but she still died young; at the age of forty-five.

Lewis' epitaph for her grave shows his profound love for her:

Here the whole world (stars, water, air,
And field, and forest, as they were
Reflected in a single mind)
Like cast off clothes was left behind

Davidson's death caused Lewis to doubt his own beliefs, something he explored in his 1961 book, *A Grief Observed*.

"Where is God?" he wrote. "Go to him when your need is desperate, when all other help is vain, and what do you find? A door slammed in your face."[45]

Lewis asked God "why?" many times after that. At the end of *A Grief Observed*, he finally concluded:

"God has not been trying an experiment on my faith or love in order to find out their quality. He knew it already. It was I who didn't. In this trial He makes us occupy the dock, the witness box, and the bench all at once. He always knew that my temple was a house of cards. His only way of making me realize the fact was to knock it down."[46]

Ultimately, we have to accept that God's answers don't depend on who we are or what we've done. Scripture also warns us against comparing our experiences to anyone else's.

At one point in the Bible, Jesus returned to Earth following his resurrection, and he spoke with Peter near the Sea of Galilee. (The same sea where Peter almost drowned when he

---

[45] C.S. Lewis, *A Grief Observed* (New York, NY: Faber and Faber, 1961).

[46] Lewis, *A Grief Observed*.

took his eyes off Christ.)

Jesus forewarned Peter that he won't die an easy death:

"But when you are old, you will stretch out your hands, and others will dress you and take you where you don't want to go."[47]

To which Peter naturally replied, and here I'm paraphrasing, "Whoa! But what about him?" And then he pointed to "the disciple Jesus loved," whom many scholars believe is John. Jesus' response is an unequivocal, "It's none of your business":

Jesus replied, "If I want him to remain alive until I return, what is that to you? As for you, follow me."[48]

As humans, it's only natural to want to know why God would answer our prayers one way, and our neighbor's prayers another way. Much like a toddler who wants to know "how come?", it's hard for us to wrap our minds around the concept of suffering and grief. And that's okay. God doesn't punish us for questioning his actions, and he doesn't get angry when we want to know why.

As for me, I've learned to accept the fact that God chose to heal me, whether or not I deserved it. I may never know why it happened, but you can bet it's one of the first questions I'll ask God when I get to heaven.

---

[47] John 21:18, NIV

[48] John 21:22, NLT

What's one "no" from God I wish I could change?

____
____
____
____

Did anything good come from that hardship? If so, what?

____
____
____
____

How can I come to terms with my situation, without comparing my life to anyone else's?

____
____
____
____

Chapter 10: PREPARING OUR HEARTS FOR PRAYER

In a way, our prayer lives are like exercise: even if we feel like we're perfectly healthy right now, the Bible counsels us to "bulk up" for when hard times hit. I've seen perfectly fit people jogging on the bayou near my home, but I know they're doing it as much for their future health as for how they feel today.

Did you know it's a scientific fact our bodies memorize the sensation of physical exercise, even after we stop doing it?

According to a recent study, which was recounted in the *Journal of Applied Physiology*, a group of test subjects was placed on an exercise regimen for eight months. Then, the group stopped exercising for two weeks and scientists tested their blood-glucose levels. Guess what? The group's blood continued to process sugar effectively, as if the people were still exercising, even when they weren't.[49]

It's the same with prayer. Although we could be cruising through life right now, enjoying the scenery, thinking nothing will ever change, everything could turn upside-down tomorrow. And it's the person who knows this—and prepares for it—who isn't caught unawares.

There's a famous country song called "Closer to You," co-written by singer Mat Kearney.[50] In it, he says we're all just "one phone call from our knees."

Maybe you've had a phone call like that. One you didn't expect, and one you wished you never had to answer. Or, maybe you received a text that announced something horrible. Perhaps someone knocked on your door with a heartrending

---

[49]Abou Asssi, et al. "The Effect of Aerobic, Resistance and Combination Training."(*Journal of Applied Physiology,* June 2015).

[50] Kearney, M. "Closer to You," *City of Black and White*. (Columbia Records, 2009).

message.

Whatever your situation, you know the feeling: your feet fall through the floor first, and then everything turns upside-down, as if you're caught in the middle of a little kid's snow globe. Once your world finally rights itself, you're left with a terrible realization: you didn't dream what just happened.

It's at times like these that our responses become automatic. Then, the thoughts, words and Bible verses we've kept in our hearts bubble to the surface. Even though we can barely remember to breathe, our minds will revert to what's stored deep inside.

The Bible tells us time and time again to develop a relationship with God first, so our response becomes automatic, no matter what the circumstances.

The psalmists were particularly good at this. Now, most of the psalms in the Bible begin with an introduction that segues from one psalm to the next. But the first two psalms are different, which is why many people think they should be read together.

They echo the same message, but on a different scale. Psalm 1 looks at the need for individuals to spend quality time with God, while Psalm 2 emphasizes how entire nations should do the same thing.

In Psalm 1, the writer praises those who follow God's will; who "meditate on it day and night."[51] The opposite is true of the wicked, who will be "condemned at the time of judgement."[52]

In Psalm 2, we see whole nations who have turned away from God.

Now then, you kings, act wisely!
Be warned, you rulers of the earth!
Serve the Lord with reverent fear,
and rejoice with trembling.[53]

---

[51] Psalm 1:2, NLT

[52] Psalm 1:5, NLT

[53] Psalm 2:10-11, NLT

The psalmist warns that nations that ignore Christ will do so at their peril. That it's only the people—and countries—who pull close to God who will find a refuge when storms come.

So, here's the first step in preparing our hearts for prayer: acknowledging we need to make it a priority, and the sooner, the better.

King David (who may or may not have written the first two psalms, depending on whom you ask), later writes about how he personally communes with God:

My heart has heard you say, "Come and talk with me," and my heart responds, "Lord, I am coming."[54]

David knew—from his earliest days as a shepherd boy to his final days as king of Israel—the only way he could make it through his trials was by spending time with God; by constantly preparing his heart for prayer.

He also knew he needed to confess his sins and get right with God before he ever bowed his head. That's another way we ready ourselves for our prayer time.

In Psalm 32 we read:

Finally, I confessed all my sins to you and stopped trying to hide my guilt.
I said to myself, "I will confess my rebellion to the Lord."
And you forgave me. All my guilt is gone! [55]

It's not that the writer—King David—saw confession as a get-out-of-jail-free card. He didn't use it to win a "yes" for all his prayers. And he wasn't saying confession was a means to an end. Instead, he was saying the opposite: that confession *is* the end; something we do to lighten our hearts so we can pray with a clean conscience.

David wrote those words and more after he'd broken one

---

[54] Psalm 27:8, NLT

[55] Psalm 32:5, NLT

of the Ten Commandments. He'd taken another man's wife for himself, and he knew he'd disappointed God:

Wash away all my iniquity and cleanse me from my sin. For I know my transgressions, and my sin is always before me.[56]

He'd just slept with Bathsheba, who was married to Uriah, one of his soldiers. But David didn't sugarcoat his sin, and he didn't try to blame it on anyone else. He knew he'd failed God, so he owned up to it, in order to approach God with a clean heart.

Which brings us to another point. Remember James 5:16, which included the word "righteous?" The first line of that verse reads:

Therefore, confess your sins to one another, and pray for one another so that you may be healed[57]

The next part raises some questions:

The effective prayer of a righteous man can accomplish much.[58]

Does that sentence bother you at all? It bothered me, at first. It seemed as if James was advocating we work our way toward heaven. That only righteous people should approach God in prayer, because those are the only people he wants to hear from.

But elsewhere in the Bible, we learn a "righteous" man (or woman) is one who is committed to doing God's will and to cultivating a relationship with him. It's not necessarily someone who is perfect, or powerful, or blameless.

---

[56] Psalm 51:2-3, NIV

[57] James 5:16, New American Standard Bible (NASB)

[58] James 5:16, NASB

According to Merriam-Webster's, the definition of righteous is: "acting in accord with divine or moral law."[59]

It was King David's son, King Solomon, who gave us a poetic description of what it meant to be righteous. He wrote these words in Proverbs:

The way of the righteous is like the first gleam of dawn,
Which shines ever brighter until the full light of day. [60]

The analogy is repeated by Daniel (who was born some five-hundred years after King Solomon), when he wrote:

Those who are wise will shine as bright as the sky
And those who lead many to righteousness will shine like the stars forever.[61]

Notice the repetition? Whenever an idea is repeated in the Bible, it's always a good idea to pay attention!

Here, Daniel was relaying a prophesy he received about the end of the world. He wrote the righteous (the wise) will be separated from the unrighteous (the unwise) with two very different outcomes.

All of which is to say that being righteous doesn't mean we're perfect. It means we're actively seeking God's will for our lives, and we're holding fast to the things God holds dear.

Elsewhere in the Bible, we're reminded that righteousness comes because of faith in Jesus, and not because of anything we've done. When we believe in him, *his* righteousness covers our transgressions. In Romans 3, Paul wrote:

This righteousness is given through faith in Jesus Christ to

---

[59] "righteous." *Merriam-Webster.com.* Merriam-Webster, 2019. https://www.merriam-webster.com.

[60] Proverbs 4:18, NASB

[61] Daniel 12:3, NASB

all who believe. [62]

Here's a disclaimer: I'd love to say I had a thriving prayer life before I got sick. Granted, I prayed every day, but it wasn't the first thing that popped into my head whenever something happened in my life.

This fact became painfully obvious when I ran into a neighbor at a local meeting in our community.

Before the meeting, I spent several minutes complaining to her about something or other. (I can't even remember the topic now.) I fully expected her to commiserate with me, or at least offer some advice. Instead, she looked me dead in the eye and asked, "Have you prayed about it yet?"

Gulp. It was quite humbling to realize she was right. Here I had the energy to complain to her, but I hadn't even thought to pray about it.

Let's look back at the singer who wrote the bestselling county song, "Closer to Love." When the song first came out in 2009, Kearney said he never thought the line about a phone call would resonate with people like it did. He said he meant to write about the difficulties people face in this world, and how one instant can change everything.

He didn't mean "one phone call from our knees" to be about prayer. But that's how Christians took it, he said, because they realized our fate lies in someone else's hands, and not in our own.

Not that we don't try to control our futures, and by any means possible. As humans, most of us do it: we adopt little rituals to prevent bad luck (remember when people carried rabbits' feet?) or to encourage good luck. (A baseball player who refuses to shave his moustache during the World Series comes to mind.)

I'm sure you've seen a horseshoe tacked over a door at one time or another. Usually, the open end of the shoe faces up. That's because people who lived during the Middle Ages were so afraid of witches, they'd do anything to keep them away. Since witches were supposedly afraid of horses,

---

[62] Romans 3:21-22, NIV

homeowners started nailing upside-down horseshoes above their doors.

Silly, wasn't it? But that was so long ago, people might say, and we're so much more sophisticated now. Oh, really? Today, architects and builders still go out of their way to mis-number the floors in skyscrapers. Most floors skip from the twelfth to the fourteenth floor, with nothing in-between.

Check out the elevator in your hotel the next time you go on vacation. Or, the one at your doctor's office when you're sick. Odds are good any high-rise building you visit will be missing a thirteenth floor, as if by magic.

Do you know why we do that? Ages ago, the Vikings made up stories about the Norse gods. In one of those stories, twelve gods were invited to eat dinner at Valhalla, which was a fancy banquet hall. But a thirteenth god crashed the party, and because of him, one of the other gods died. Ever since then, people have avoided Friday the 13th; the thirteenth floor in high-rises; and the number thirteen in addresses. All in a quest to control the future.

Which brings us to another point: apart from developing a habit of prayer and confessing our sins, another way to prepare our hearts for prayer is to acknowledge who's really in charge.

Many Bible verses bear this out:

Our God is in the heavens; he does all that he pleases.[63]

Many are the plans in the mind of a man, but it is the purpose of the Lord that will stand. [64]

These verses point to the omniscience of God, and to the fact we can do nothing apart from him.

Even Jonah knew this was the case. The reluctant prophet had done everything he could to avoid preaching to the nasty Ninevites. After he almost drowned in the sea, God sent a fish

---

[63] Psalm 115:3, ESV

[64] Proverbs 19:21, ESV

to save him, and he lived in the belly of that fish for three days and three nights. By that time, Jonah realized his plans were *not* the ones that mattered. In Jonah 2, we read:

> *As my life was slipping away, I remembered the Lord.*
> *And my earnest prayer went out to you in your holy temple.*
> *Those who worship false gods turn their backs on all God's mercies.*
> *But I will offer sacrifices to you with songs of praise,*
> *And I will fulfill all my vows.*
> *For my salvation comes from the Lord alone.*[65]

Once we realize we should make prayer a priority; we should confess our sins in order to pray with a clean heart; and we should always remember who's in charge; there's a final way we can prepare our hearts for prayer. Surprisingly, it has nothing to do with what we see, feel or say. It's something that goes against the grain of what it means to be human, because God created us to be thinking, feeling, expressive beings.

That "something" is silence.

Huh? Doesn't that go against the whole idea of praying? Aren't we supposed to cry out to God, like David did?

> *The righteous cry, and the Lord heareth, and delivereth them out of all their troubles.*[66]

How can God hear us if we don't speak, or if we don't cry out to him? Apart from the fact God already knows what's in our hearts before we ever utter a word, there's one thing we often fail at: listening.

As humans, we're so accustomed to noise and distraction that silence can bother us. Have you ever noticed how people react during a power outage, when they're forced to give up their computers, their television sets, their distractions?

---

[65] Jonah 2:7-9, NLB

[66] Psalm 34:17, NIV

We don't have to look too far back in history to find out what happens. On August 11, 1996, several power lines in California came into contact with trees. That, combined with triple-digit temperatures, caused a power outage that ultimately affected seven states, along with parts of Canada and Mexico.

Overall, the blackout affected 7.5 million people. Some people lost electricity for only a few minutes, while others suffered for six days. During that time, many residents didn't have access to telephones (if they had a cell phone, it was a chunky flip-phone, since smartphones were still ten years away), and they couldn't even watch television. According to researchers who studied the blackout, one of the greatest public health issues didn't come from contaminated water, or from spoiled food. It came from the social isolation that people experienced.

We all need to talk. Most of us are born to talk. But, sometimes, it is in the silence that we get the most out of our prayer time.

Mother Teresa—who was surrounded by the cacophony of hospital wards and needy throngs her entire life—understood this better than many people. In her 2010 book, she wrote:

In the silence of the heart God speaks… Souls of prayer are souls of great silence.[67]

She went on to tell a story about a certain priest she knew:

…I said to him, "Father, you talk all day about God. How close you must be to God!" And do you know what he said to me? He said, "I may be talking much about God, but I may be talking very little to God."

In other words, the priest understood that he couldn't hear

---

[67] Mother Theresa, *In the Heart of the World: Thoughts, Stories and Prayers*. (New World Library, March 2010).

from God unless he practiced silence. How will we ever know what God wants of us if we don't pause long enough to listen to him?

In the end, preparing our hearts for prayer should involve confessing our sins, so we can approach God's throne with a clean conscience; recognizing God alone is in charge of our fates; and remaining silent long enough to listen to him. Those are some of the key points given to us by Mother Teresa and others...keys that unlock the door to powerful prayers.

What is one way I can prepare my heart for prayer?

____
____
____
____

Is there any unacknowledged sin in my life that could impact my prayer time?

____
____
____
____

Do I welcome silence? If not…why not?

____
____
____
____

Chapter 11: PREPARING OTHERS FOR OUR PRAYERS

If you're like me, you get asked to pray for people all the time. The requests may be impersonal, through the anonymity of social media, or very personal, through private conversations.

Either way, it can be overwhelming to remember so many prayer requests. And at times like that, it's easy to toss off "I'll pray for you" when it's our turn to say something. After all, it sounds good, right? It sounds like we're actually doing something, with the added bonus that our requestor may not ever find out if we kept our word.

So, what's the problem? On the one hand, it allows people to know you're praying for them, which might give them courage to face whatever trial or adversity they're going through. On the other hand, though, it can be a platitude, as phony and plastic as "have a nice day." Something to make it sound like we're doing something, when we really aren't.

When Hurricane Harvey hit Houston in 2017, it swamped whole neighborhoods with dirty, disease-ridden water. People couldn't get into their flooded homes; they lost basic utilities like electricity and telephone service; and workplaces shuttered when employees couldn't navigate the roads.

The prayer requests piled up. While I tried to pray for everyone who asked, I probably forgot as many of those needs as I remembered, if I'm being honest. At the end of the day, there was only so much time and energy to go around, and so many people affected by the storm.

That's when I started questioning whether saying "I'll pray for you" actually did more harm than good. Was I really helping the people who asked me to pray for them, or was I helping myself out of an uncomfortable silence?

Now, some people believe there's nothing wrong with telling people, "I'll pray for you." The Billy Graham Evangelistic Association falls squarely into that camp. Here's what they have to say about it:

...almost everyone who's facing a serious need (whether it is an illness or some other difficulty) will be encouraged by knowing someone is praying for them. Even if they've never given much thought to God, they know they may be in grave danger and will welcome the prayers of others.

Likewise, people point to the example of Paul as someone who told people he'd pray for them. He even went so far as to provide a laundry list of all the things he hoped God would give the people of Philippi when he wrote to them in Philippians 1:

And this is my prayer: that your love may abound more and more in knowledge and depth of insight, so that you may be able to discern what is best and may be pure and blameless for the day of Christ, filled with the fruit of righteousness that comes through Jesus Christ—to the glory and praise of God.[68]

Paul framed his remarks in an "if this/then that" format. He told them if God granted his prayer for them to love each other with wisdom and insight, *then* they'd have discernment about the best way to live, and *then* they'd be blameless when Christ returned. He attributed everything to the work of God, and nothing to what he'd done.

Why do you think he did that? Couldn't Paul just make a blanket statement about praying for the people of Philippi, and leave it at that?

Maybe because the people to whom he was writing already had prayed for him, and he was grateful for their support. Here's what he said toward the end of the first chapter:

...for I know that through your prayers and God's provision of the Spirit of Jesus Christ what has happened to me will turn

---

[68] Philippians 1:9-11, NIV

out for my deliverance.[69]

It's safe to say Paul also falls into the camp of people who believe there's nothing wrong with announcing our intentions to pray for someone. Why, even God announced a forthcoming prayer when he spoke to Job's friends:

...My servant Job will pray for you, and I will accept his prayer on your behalf.[70]

That's because the friends had so angered God, he couldn't listen to *their* prayers. He could only abide the prayers of someone righteous, like Job. (This was before Christ came and took away our sins on the cross.)

But how does that jibe with what Jesus had to say about prayer in the New Testament? In Matthew, Jesus specifically counseled *against* making a big show out of our prayers:

And when you pray, do not be like the hypocrites, for they love to pray standing in the synagogues and on the street corners to be seen by men. I tell you the truth, they have received their reward in full.[71]

He repeated that sentiment in Luke, where he warned people about showboating during their prayers:

Beware of the scribes, who like to walk around in long robes, and love greetings in the marketplaces and the best seats in the synagogues and the places of honor at feasts, who devour widows' houses and for a pretense make long prayers. They will receive the greater condemnation[72]

---

[69] Philippians 1:19-27, NIV

[70] Job 42:8, NLT

[71] Matthew 6:5, NIV

[72] Luke 20:46, NIV

Here, Jesus seemed to be repeating the idea that we should pray for others quietly and with a minimum of fuss. But maybe that's because Jesus had always been more concerned about *why* people prayed than *how* they were praying.

During his time on earth, Jesus warned people time and again that God sees through our phoniness. After all, he made our hearts, so he knows what's inside them. The two verses mentioned here slay the idea that we can pull anything over on God.

If you've been a Christian for any length of time, you know there are certain "buzzwords" when it comes to prayer. We don't ask God for wisdom; we ask for "discernment." We don't want God to protect our loved ones; we request a "hedge of protection."

Let's call these things what they really are: clichés. Most of us use them, whether we want to admit it or not. Like a good actor who knows his lines, we find ourselves spouting great-sounding phrases, instead of speaking from our hearts.

These "Christian clichés" can be harmful for several reasons: they allow us to slide through our prayer time with minimal thought, like a robot programmed with the right code, and they can create distance between us and the people who don't know this special language.

Worse, it can make us sound flip, when that's the last thing that's needed after someone has poured out her heart to us.

That's the kind of showmanship Jesus accused the scribes and pharisees of performing. It's one thing to say, "I'll pray for you," but whenever we say, "I'll cover you with prayer," it's time to ask ourselves whether we're speaking for the other person's benefit, or ours. Whether we're out to make ourselves look better, which is what got the scribes and pharisees into trouble in the first place, or if we intend to carry through with our promise.

These clichés even extend to popular Christian sayings, unfortunately. Remember the bracelets, coffee mugs and bumper stickers that asked, What Would Jesus Do? We know Jesus was without sin, even though the scriptures say he was tempted in all things (Hebrews 4:15), but we can't know for certain what Jesus would do in every situation, since we're not lucky enough to have him with us. We can only look at what he did in the past, and then surmise what he'd do in the future. Maybe a better question would have been, "What has Jesus Done?"

In the end, phrases like that, or "secret prayer words," can separate us from the very people we want to connect with.

That's why I've adopted a third choice. I saw it firsthand when people visited my room at the hospital, or they wrote notes to my inbox. Instead of saying a blanket "I'll pray for you," or not saying anything at all, these people would tell me specifically what they were going to ask God to do on my behalf.

My sister kept a journal for visitors to sign, and they'd also write which specific things they intended to pray for. Here are some of my favorites:

We're praying ***urgently*** *(their emphasis, not mine) that God will bring healing to your kidneys and lungs.*

I pray the doctors will be surprised by how quickly you will recover.

I am begging God to put ***his*** *(again, her emphasis) breath in your lungs and heal your infection.*

Those are specific things these people prayed for, and not general, blanket statements that could be applied to anyone in need of prayer. This told me two things: they'd thought about my particular situation, and they probably wouldn't forget what they'd promised to do.

I also loved it when people prayed specific Bible verses over me. These are some of the ones people prayed over me in the hospital:

I lift my eyes to the hills. From where does my strength come? My strength comes from the Lord, the maker of heaven and earth.[73]

---

[73] Psalm 121:1-2, ESV

Heal me (here she inserted my name) Lord, and I will be healed.
Save me and I will be saved.[74]

Peace I leave with you
My peace I give you.
I do not give to you as the world gives.
Let not your heart be troubled and do not be afraid[75]

This is the way I approach my prayer life now. Whenever someone asks me to pray for them, I ask them what, specifically, they need help with. Not only does it encourage people to know their particular needs are being remembered, but it reminds me when I physically hear the words escape my lips. "Oh, yeah. I promised (fill in the blank) I would ask God to (blank)."

That's the way I intend to prepare other people for my prayers, as long as they continue to ask for them.

---

[74] Jeremiah 17:14, ESV

[75] John 14:27, NIV

What are three specific needs I can pray for today?

____

What are some questions I can ask people before I pray for them?

What does Jesus say about the way we should approach others' prayer requests?

Chapter 12: UNSEEN MIRACLES

Many years ago, my family and I visited a place in Washington, D.C. called the International Spy Museum. Just like the name suggests, the museum held everything related to spying—from teeny-tiny cameras the Germans attached to pigeons during World War I to something called the lipstick pistol, which Russians employed during the Cold War.

I read something during that visit I'll never forget. One placard described how the CIA thwarted hundreds of terrorist plots every day meant to hurt Americans. Yet, no one in our country ever learned about them, because the CIA kept its activities secret. Some of those plots were simple, while others involved large-scale operations that could've resulted in massive destruction.

As Americans, we go about our days in relative safety, not realizing the reason for that safety lies in an organization charged with protecting us, sight unseen.

The same is true of God. How many times does God protect us during the day, yet we don't even realize it? We may pray for something we think we want, and then we'll complain when we don't see the prayer automatically answered. Often, it's not that he hasn't answered our prayer, but that he's performing unseen miracles that are even better for us than anything we could imagine.

Ironically, Satan himself knows God is in the business of protecting us surreptitiously. Before Satan undertook a plan of destruction for Job, a wealthy rancher and property owner in the Old Testament, he first complained to God that Job had a "wall of protection around him":

Satan replied to the Lord, "Yes, but Job has good reason to fear God. You have always put a wall of protection around him and his home and his property."[76]

---

[76] Job 1:9-10, NLT

Satan asked God to lift this wall so he could attack Job to test his faith. Even Satan recognized that when God chose to protect someone, nothing Satan or anyone else did could change that.

Just one fascinating way God protected his people occurred during the Six-Day War, which took place between June 5 and June 10 in 1967. Israel faced so many enemies, everyone assumed she'd be destroyed outright. But, as we see throughout the Bible, Israel holds a special place in God's heart.

Prior to the war, Jerusalem was split in two, with half falling under the control of Israel's neighbor to the east, Jordan. On May 15, 1967, Egypt, Israel's neighbor to the south, began amassing weapons in the Sinai Peninsula. A week later, Egypt closed the Straits of Tiran to Israeli vehicles, which Israel considered an act of war.

It looked as if Israel was impossibly outnumbered. No fewer than seven of its neighbors threatened to overrun the country: Egypt, Jordan, Syria, Iraq, Kuwait, Algeria and Lebanon. Combined, they had half a million troops (about twice as many as Israel); twice the number of tanks; and four times the number of aircraft. They also had the backing of the mighty Soviet Union.

Sound a little like David and Goliath? But, like David, Israel had one big plus on its side: God.

Throughout the Bible, God has protected Israel, and especially Jerusalem. The city is named eight-hundred times in the Bible; more than any other city.

In Zechariah 12, the Old Testament prophet provided this vision for Israel's future:

In that day shall the Lord defend the inhabitants of Jerusalem; and he that is feeble among them at that day shall be as David; and the house of David shall be as God, as the angel of the Lord before them.[77]

---

[77] Zechariah 12:8, KJV

The world waited as May 1967 dragged on, wondering what would become of God's most-treasured nation. If there was any question as to the motive of her neighbors for gathering their troops, Iraq's president summed it up succinctly. In a speech he gave on May 31 of that year, Abdul Rahman Arif said, "The existence of Israel is an error which must be rectified. This is our opportunity to wipe out the ignominy which has been with us since 1948. Our goal is clear—to wipe Israel off the map."

What happened next is a testament to God's faithfulness. On June 5, 1967, two-hundred Israeli Air Force planes were heading toward Egypt and its air bases. Even though Israel's pilots flew low to avoid being spotted, a Jordanian radar facility noticed an unusual amount of aircraft activity near the sea and sent this message of warning to Egypt: "ibd."

That acronym stood for "inbound," which was Jordan's way of warning Egypt that Israel was on its way.

However, Egypt had changed its coding frequencies the day before, and they neglected to inform Jordan. Egypt had so much anti-aircraft ammunition ready, it could've easily destroyed the Israeli fighter pilots, had it known about the raid. But it never ordered its munitions deployed, because it never received the message from Jordan.

That day, Israel destroyed half of Egypt's air force, or two-hundred and four planes, most of which were parked in the Sinai Desert and waiting to be deployed.

That's just one example of how God has answered prayers by not allowing something to happen. He maneuvered behind the scenes to protect his people, which no one knew about at the time. He could've easily sent fire from heaven to rain down on Egypt's troops, or done something equally showy, but he opted to use the power of his unseen strength instead.

A more current example happened here in America, in the nineteen-eighties. Everyone knows country music singer Garth Brooks as the man who co-wrote a country music classic: "Unanswered Prayers."[78]

---

[78] Alger, P., Bastian, L., Brooks, G. "Unanswered Prayers." *No Fences*. (Capitol Nashville, 1990).

The song tells the story of a man who attended a football game at his former high school with his wife. While there, he ran across an ex-girlfriend, whom he always planned to marry one day. In fact, he prayed for that to happen, and when it didn't, he couldn't understand why God said no to the prayer.

Only when he returned to his alma mater with his wife did he realize God had been working on his behalf the entire time. Instead of answering the man's immediate request, God allowed the girl to break up with him, because God knew something better was in store.

Within a year, the song reached the top spot on the "Billboard Hot Country Songs" chart, and Brooks began telling interviewers the reason he felt compelled to write it.

According to Brooks, he and his wife returned to Oklahoma in 1989. While there, he ran into a girl he had dated while a student at Yukon High School. Brooks said he remembered asking God to one day make that girl his wife. And, just like in the song, Brooks realized if God had granted that request, he never would've met his wife, the woman he loved and lived with for more than fifteen years.

Let's end with a final example of God's unseen hand, which happened not long ago. It was a miracle many people missed, because they were so enthralled by the flashy outer story, they failed to see the quieter miracle underneath it.

As reported by ABC News, Britain's *Daily Mail* and others, motorist Katie Lentz, 19, was struck head-on by a drunk driver in Missouri on August 4, 2013. The young woman was traveling on a lonely stretch of Highway 19, near Center, Missouri, at nine o'clock that morning.

First responders tried for more than an hour and a half to free Katie from her car. When their efforts failed, she asked those first responders to pray with her. She thought all hope was lost, and she would die on that lonely road.

At that moment, someone else joined them. It was a priest in his liturgical collar, and he volunteered to pray with Katie and anoint her with oil.

Once the priest finished, he left again; as mysteriously as he had arrived. When the Hannibal (Missouri) Fire Department appeared and tried to extricate Katie from the wreckage afterward, they were able to finally free her from the car and airlift her to a nearby ICU.

Not surprisingly, the Internet went crazy. Everyone speculated on the mysterious stranger who prayed over Katie. Was he an angel? Someone the rescuers only imagined they saw? No one remembered the priest approaching the car, and no one saw him leave, but everyone swore he prayed over the injured girl.

The truth was far less dramatic, but no less amazing. Reverend Patrick Dowling was performing the eight-thirty mass nearby when he passed the blocked road that led to Katie's accident. Workers had secured the scene for a quarter mile in every direction, but Rev. Dowling said he felt God nudging him to continue down the road, to where he'd find the injured girl.

When the priest came forward a week later and admitted he was the one who ministered to Katie after the accident, people were disappointed. It wasn't an angel after all, but a flesh-and-blood man who performed an ordinary Catholic prayer, albeit with extraordinary results.

What many people didn't know—because the media dropped the story after that—was that Reverend Dowling was never supposed to be anywhere near the road that morning. He was assigned to a different parish, but he received a call from a sick priest, who asked him to perform mass in his absence.

Reverend Dowling later said it was the first time he'd ever traveled down that road. For some reason, he felt compelled to drive down the lonely stretch of highway, and then to continue around the barricades, although he didn't know why at the time.

If God can work out details like that for one of his children—a teenager critically injured on a lonely road in the Midwest—imagine all the other ways he has worked behind the scenes for us.

Interestingly, the priest appeared at the exact moment when Katie said she'd given up hope. She said she asked the first responders to pray with her because she thought she was going to die. And that's the moment God sent someone to calm her spirit and strengthen her resolve.

Are you waiting for a dramatic sign from God that he's

heard your prayer? Something larger than life, so you'll have no doubts? It doesn't always work like that. Sometimes, it's the unseen hand of God working in the background that brings about change. If we only knew everything he was doing on our behalf, we'd no doubt be amazed.

What are some of the ways God has protected me and my family in the past, only we didn't know it at the time?

____
____
____
____

How does that change the way I view "unanswered" prayer requests?

____
____
____
____

What can I do to bolster my faith that God is working all things together for my good? (Romans 8:28)

____
____
____
____

Chapter 13: ENDNOTES–SPECIAL PRAYERS FOR SPECIAL TIMES

No matter where you are in your prayer life, I hope the people and stories you've read about here have inspired you. At the end of the day, it's all about understanding the power of prayer to connect us with the one who created us.

Sometimes, we can see famous prayers in a new light by looking at the backgrounds of the people who wrote them. That way, we can better understand why people felt compelled to write the prayers they did.

Usually, those are the prayers that resonate most with us, because the singers/Nobel Prize winners/politicians have brought a special backstory to the prayer's creation.

Over the years, many singers have recorded a song called "Oh Lord, You're Beautiful." Everyone from Michael W. Smith to Rebecca St. James has made the song a bestseller. One of the verses contains a powerful prayer, especially given the history of its author:

I want to take your word and shine it all around
But first, help me to just live it, Lord.[79]

The person who wrote that song was Keith Green, a singer/songwriter who lived and worked some forty years ago. Green never set out to be a Christian composer and singer. In fact, he wanted to be a rock star, and he had the pedigree to make that happen.

His grandfather was a composer who started a music label called Jaguar Records, and his mother trained to be a singer at Carnegie Hall. By the time he was five, Green started piano and voice lessons; by nine he was writing his own songs. A

---

[79] Green, Keith. "Oh Lord, You're Beautiful." *So You Wanna Go Back to Egypt*. (Universal Music Publishing, 1980).

mere two years later, he became the youngest person ever to sign with the American Society of Composers, Authors, and Publishers (ASCAP).

Things kept rolling right along, and it looked like Green was on his way to pop stardom. He signed with Decca Records at the age of eleven (the same year he became a member of ASCAP) and he released his first pop single that year. He wrote ten more songs by the time he was twelve, he appeared in *Time* magazine, and he performed on several national TV shows.

Sort of makes you feel unaccomplished, right? By the time I was twelve, I wanted nothing more than to meet Bobby Sherman (ask your mother) and read my *Tiger Beat* magazines in peace. I *didn't* compose music, and I sure didn't have the talent to sing before a national audience.

But, amazingly, everything fell apart for Green after that. Another teen sensation called Donny Osmond (again, ask your mother!) came on the scene and started eating away at Green's audience. His record label dropped him the following year, and he was considered a "has-been" by the ripe old age of fourteen.

Without his dream, Green fell apart. He ran away from home, and then he turned to drugs to fill the hole in his heart. He thought he'd never sing again, and his life was over before it'd really begun.

But then, something wonderful happened. Green became a Christian in his early twenties and felt God calling him to sing again. He returned to the stage, but this time as a Christian artist.

Green wasn't your typical performer, though. He often gave away free tickets to his concerts, and he'd include a free cassette (this was long before the days of CDs) with every one purchased, so buyers could give it to their non-Christian friends.

When he wrote about his desire to live his Christian faith, he took it to heart. He and his wife opened their home to drug addicts, prostitutes and runaways in the late '80s, and they ended up renting five extra houses in their neighborhood for people to use. The prayer in "Oh Lord, You're Beautiful" resonated so deeply with Green, he and his wife started "Last

Days Ministries," with plans to operate a forty-acre ranch in Texas for people living on the fringe.

Unfortunately, Green never got to see that dream become reality, because he died in a single-engine plane crash in 1982, when he was only twenty-eight years old. But his songs live on, including "Oh Lord, You're Beautiful," which new singers seem to rediscover every few years.

Almost forty years before Green's death, another highly accomplished person wrote a prayer that has stood the test of time. Earlier, theoretical physicist Max Planck earned the Nobel Prize for his work in a little something called the quantum theory. Basically, Planck challenged common assumptions about the make-up of atomic and subatomic particles as they related to radiation. He devised a formula that linked the energy of radiation to its frequency, for which he won the Nobel Prize for Physics in 1918.

Many people don't realize some of the scientists mentioned on the popular television series *The Big Bang Theory* actually were Christians. While the lead character, Sheldon Cooper, professed to be an atheist, some of his scientific idols, including Sir Isaac Newton and Planck, believed in God.

Planck was German, and he spent World War II in his homeland, although he didn't agree with Hitler and the Nazis. In 1944, his home in Berlin was destroyed in an air raid, and he lost all his scientific papers and correspondence. Worse than that, his son Erwin was arrested for his role in a plot to kill Adolph Hitler. After Erwin was tried by a kangaroo court and found guilty of treason, he was hanged in a Berlin prison.

Planck was devasted. Here he'd lost his son and his home, not to mention all his scientific papers. Nevertheless, he wrote a prayer to one of his friends, the German professor and publisher Anton Kippenberg:

"If there is consolation anywhere it is in the eternal, and I consider it a grace of heaven that belief in the eternal has been rooted deeply in me since childhood.

May God protect and strengthen you for everything that still may come, before this insanity in which we are forced to live reaches its end."

The more Planck studied science, the more he became convinced God created the world and everything in it. In one of his lectures, he famously declared that, "Both religion and science require a belief in God. For believers, God is in the beginning, and for physicists, He is at the end of all considerations."[80]

A final example of a special prayer given during a special time comes to us from the sixteenth President of the United States. Abraham Lincoln's life was far from easy, as we all know. He was born to a dirt-poor farmer in Kentucky, and Abraham only attended school in fits and starts as a child. (About a year altogether.) His father moved the family to Indiana when Lincoln was eight, and the boy spent his days clearing land, planting crops and building a cabin for the family instead of attending school. Then, when he was nine, his mother died and his eleven-year-old sister took over the household duties.

Despite this, Lincoln somehow taught himself to read and write, and he borrowed books from neighbors to learn about things like history, poetry and science.

Once he became President, Lincoln led a nation that teetered on the brink of civil war. He won the election in November 1860, but by March, when he was formally inaugurated, seven states decided to pull out of the Union to form the Confederate States of America. The following month, the Confederates fired on Fort Sumter in South Carolina, and the nation plunged into war.

While the Confederate leader was a West Point graduate and former Secretary of War, Lincoln had to teach himself how to command the armed forces. During this time, he often attended a weekly prayer meeting held at New York Avenue Presbyterian Church, which was close to the White House. (You can still visit the church, and it offers tours after Sunday services.)

Instead of sitting in full view, though, Lincoln chose to sit in

---

[80] Planck, M. "Religion and Natural Science." (Lecture given in 1937).

the pastor's study and crack the door open. According to Dr. Phineas D. Gurley, the church's pastor, Lincoln didn't want anyone to be distracted from their prayers by his presence.

He famously told a friend during this time: "I have been driven many times upon my knees by the overwhelming conviction that I had nowhere else to go."

And still, the war raged on. After Union forces won the Battle of Gettysburg in 1863, a general asked Lincoln if he worried about the outcome beforehand. He replied:

"...when everybody seemed panic-stricken, and nobody could tell what was going to happen, oppressed by the gravity of our affairs, I went to my room one day, and I locked the door, and I got down on my knees before Almighty God. And after that (I don't know how it was, and I can't explain it), soon a sweet comfort crept into my soul that God Almighty had taken the whole business into his own hands."

By the time Lincoln was re-elected in 1864, between 640,000 and 700,000 men (depending on the source) were dead, which was two percent of the population. Many others suffered devastating injuries.

At his second inaugural address in 1865, Lincoln said:

"Fondly do we hope, fervently do we pray, that this mighty scourge of war may speedily pass away. Yet if God wills that it continues...so still it must be said that the judgments of the Lord are true and righteous altogether."

Can you imagine hearing those words from a President today? While Lincoln grieved for the families that lost their sons during the war, he acknowledged the fate of America rested in God's hands, and no one else's.

Finally, the Civil War ended a month after his inaugural speech, and an assassin's bullet ended Lincoln's life only five days later.

In the end, the very best example of a special prayer—which can be prayed at *any* time and during *any* circumstance—comes to us from Jesus himself. Jesus gave the Lord's Prayer twice in the New Testament: once during the Sermon on the Mount in Matthew (a longer version), and again in Luke, when he was with his disciples.

The first three points in the Matthew prayer talk specifically about God. As many scholars have pointed out, the Bible is full of "threes," including the Trinity, the wise men, and Peter's denial of Christ in the Garden of Gethsemane.

The prayer begins with praise for the one who gave us the ability to pray in the first place:

Our Father which art in heaven, hallowed be thy name.

Thy kingdom come, Thy will be done in earth, as it is in heaven.

Give us this day our daily bread. And forgive us our debts, as we forgive our debtors.

And lead us not into temptation, but deliver us from evil:

For thine is the kingdom, and the power, and the glory, for ever and ever. Amen[81]

C.S. Lewis, whom we've already read about several times, gave his thoughts on why the prayer begins like it does. In his book, *Letters to Malcom: Chiefly on Prayer*, Lewis wrote:

Jesus taught us to address God where he is, that is, in heaven and not yet here on earth.[82]

He went on to say while God wanted to be with us, that wouldn't happen until the end of the world. For now, we need to recognize our separation from God, but we can rejoice in knowing it won't last forever.

Whole books have been written about the Lord's Prayer, and experts have analyzed every letter, word and line. Suffice it to say Jesus had a specific reason for delivering this example of the perfect prayer at the time he did.

Jesus gave the prayer for the first time during the Sermon on the Mount. He was teaching both his disciples and the crowd at large about the new order of things, now that he'd come to earth.

---

[81] Matthew 6:9-13, KJV

[82] Lewis, C.S. *Letters to Malcolm: Chiefly on Prayer.* (Harcourt, Brace & World, Inc., 1964).

Before, Jewish law was full of rules and punishments, but Jesus' message was all about grace. In fact, the last verse in the Old Testament ends with a curse:

Look, I am sending you the prophet Elijah before the great and dreadful day of the Lord arrives. His preaching will turn the hearts of fathers to their children, and the hearts of children to their fathers. Otherwise I will come and strike the land with a curse.[83]

But the Sermon on the Mount begins with blessings, or what we call the Beatitudes:

Blessed are the poor in spirit, for theirs is the kingdom of heaven.[84]

It helps to remember the timeframe of the Lord's Prayer, too. While it transcends generations and situations, the prayer was delivered in a time that looked a lot different from ours. The people in Jesus' audience didn't have access to the Internet, or whole libraries full of books, or even notepads they could write on. Back then, most people were forced to memorize someone's words if they wanted to refer back to them. So, Jesus provided a prayer that was clear, concise and easy to memorize.

The idea of "on earth as it is in heaven" struck a special chord with John Wesley, the man we discussed in Chapter 6. Wesley believed Jesus was instructing people to behave like the angels in this prayer, and to obey God like they did…willingly. In his commentary on the Bible, which Wesley wrote between 1754 and 1765, he noted:

May all the inhabitants of the earth do thy will as willingly

---

[83] Malachi 4:6, NLT

[84] Matthew 5:3, NIV

as the holy angels: may these do it continually…[85]

It's a wonderful visual of how things will be when we finally find ourselves before God. In heaven, where no one is tempted, and no one succumbs to temptation. Where the angels willingly and joyfully follow God's will, in harmony with him.

The second version of the Lord's Prayer, which is found in Luke, includes everything but the later references to God's power and glory:

And he said unto them, when ye pray, say, Our Father which art in heaven,

Hallowed be thy name. Thy kingdom come. Thy will be done, as in heaven, so in earth.

Give us day by day our daily bread.

And forgive us our sins; for we also forgive every one that is indebted to us. And lead us not into temptation; but deliver us from evil.[86]

Jesus provided the prayer in Luke after his disciples asked him point-blank how he wanted them to pray. The disciples knew John the Baptist had taught his own followers how to pray, and they wanted Jesus to do the same thing for them:

One day Jesus was praying in a certain place. When he finished, one of his disciples said to him, "Lord, teach us to pray, just as John taught his disciples."[87]

While the Bible doesn't tell us what prayer John the Baptist gave to his followers, we do know those men and women were devout. Even before the Lord's Prayer, someone asked

---

[85] Wesley, J. *Explanatory Notes Upon the New Testament* (originally published 1755 by William Bower).

[86] Luke 11:2-4, KJV

[87] Luke 11:1, NIV

Jesus why his disciples looked different than John the Baptist's:

One day, some people said to Jesus, "John the Baptist's disciples fast and pray regularly, and so do the disciples of the Pharisees. Why are your disciples always eating and drinking?[88]

To which Jesus basically replied, because I'm here with them now, and they have all the time in the world to do that once I'm gone.

Finally, there's been some discussion over what Jesus meant by our "daily bread." Some people take the words literally: they believe we should ask God to fulfill our daily needs, including the need for food.

But other people believe Jesus was talking about himself in that instance. More than once, Jesus is called "the bread of life" in the Bible, not to mention "the living bread." These people believe we should ask God to help us make Jesus a priority in our day-to-day life. They bolster this position by noting Jesus told people not to be concerned with their everyday needs later in the Sermon on the Mount:

...I tell you not to worry about everyday life—whether you have enough food and drink, or enough clothes to wear. Isn't life more than food, and your body more than clothing?[89]

---

[88] Luke 5:33, NLT

[89] Matthew 6:25, NLT

Whichever version you believe, the Lord's Prayer teaches us to include some important things when we pray: we are to acknowledge God's sovereignty; we should willingly follow his plan for our life; we should extend grace to others, just like we've been given grace; and we should ask for God's help to stay away from sin.

Whether you pray the Lord's Prayer for your daily devotional, or you personalize your prayers to reflect your life and the lives of others, I hope you've found encouragement in this book to continue making prayer a priority.

If you've never made prayer a priority in your life, I hope that changes.

Other titles from Higher Ground Books & Media:

Wise Up to Rise Up by Rebecca Benston

A Path to Shalom by Steen Burke

For His Eyes Only by John Salmon, Ph.D.

Miracles: I Love Them by Forest Godin

32 Days with Christ's Passion by Mark Etter

Knowing Affliction and Doing Recovery by John Baldasare

Out of Darkness by Stephen Bowman

Breaking the Cycle by Willie Deeanjlo White

Healing in God's Power by Yvonne Green

Chronicles of a Spiritual Journey by Stephen Shepherd

The Real Prison Diaries by Judy Frisby

My Name is Sam…And Heaven is Still Shining Through by Joe Siccardi

Add these titles to your collection today!

http://www.highergroundbooksandmedia.com

Do you have a story to tell?

Higher Ground Books & Media is an independent Christian-based publisher specializing in stories of triumph! Our purpose is to empower, inspire, and educate through the sharing of personal experiences.

Please visit our website for our submission guidelines.

http://www.highergroundbooksandmedia.com

Made in the
USA
Columbia, SC

79897613R00071

Chapter 5: WHAT PRAYER ISN'T

At one time, I thought prayer was all about mild-mannered humility. A time to gently approach God's throne, thank him profusely for his faithfulness, and then timidly ask for something. The more aw-shucks bashfulness on my part the better, because who was I to ask God for anything?

I don't think that anymore. While it's true we need to approach God reverently for the king and creator he is, I now realize he expects us to confidently state the case for what we want, and why.

I came to that conclusion after speaking with a certain friend. While a lot of people let me know they were praying for me when the pulmonologist put me on life support, this woman explained she *fought* for me with prayer.

Huh? She fought for me with prayer? That sounded wrong, for some reason. As if prayer was supposed to be more genteel than that. How could she replace something positive (prayer) with something negative (fighting) and expect anything good to come of it?

But that's how Jesus taught his disciples to pray. In Luke 11, as he's making his way to Jerusalem, where he knows he's going to be crucified, the disciples approach him for a final lesson in how to pray.

Then, teaching them more about prayer, he used this story: "Suppose you went to a friend's house at midnight, wanting to borrow three loaves of bread. You say to him, 'A friend of mine has just arrived for a visit, and I have nothing for him to eat.' And suppose he calls out from his bedroom, 'Don't bother me. The door is locked for the night, and my family and I are all in bed. I can't help you.' But I tell you this—though he won't do it for friendship's sake, if you keep knocking long enough, he will get up and give you whatever you need because of your shameless persistence.[8]

Read those words again…shameless persistence. That's how Jesus instructed his disciples to approach prayer.

The Miriam-Webster dictionary defines shameless as "being insensible to disgrace." In other words, it's when we don't care how others perceive us. Everyone could tell us to stop, but we persist in doing something anyway, because it just doesn't matter to us.

The first step, then, is to recognize our prayer time for what it really is: a fight for ourselves or for someone else.

One of Reverend Billy Graham's favorite stories involved a missionary by the name of John G. Paton. Paton was a Presbyterian missionary in the South Pacific in the mid-eighteen-hundreds. He'd moved to the island of Tanna to preach, which is about twelve-hundred miles off the coast of Australia. He'd also brought along a brand-new bride, Mary, whom he'd wed only two weeks before.

While the idea of moving to a beach in the South Pacific with your new bride, complete with swaying palm trees, sugar-white sand and crystal-clear tidepools sounds idyllic, the reality was much different. John and Mary landed in the middle of a colony of cannibals who wanted nothing more than to do away with their unwanted guests.

On one of their first nights in Tanna, a group of cannibals surrounded the Paton's new home. Imagine their terror when they looked out glassless windows and saw men wearing necklaces fashioned from human bones. Rather than arm themselves with clubs or torches, though, the Patons fell to their knees to pray. And not for a few minutes…they prayed all night long. They prayed with shameless persistence.

When morning finally dawned and the cannibals dispersed, John and Mary rose from their knees. Not a hair on their heads had been touched, although the cannibals had every chance—and every intention—to kill them.

About a year later, John Paton brought one of the cannibals' two chiefs to Christ. He had a question for the man,

---

[8] Luke 11:5–8, NLT